ITALIA, NEW CO...
...ERSEA DOGS...
...NDARD, NATURA...
...TEXTILE MUSEUM, N...
...UL'S CATHEDRAL, DO...
...RISTIE'S, FORTNUM &...
...SWEETINGS, TOWE...
...OSPITAL, BAR ITALIA...
...WEMBLEY STADIUM...
...ESTY'S THEATRE, NE...
...SAUDS, EVENING ST...
...TER HOTEL, BEIGEL...
...DEN MARKET, BAR...
...ORY MUSEUM, REFO...
...OLLEGE HOSPITAL...
...IDGE, ROUNDHOUSE...
...ARD, REGENT'S PAR...

LONDON LIVES

LONDON LIVES

24 iconic people and places around the clock

DANNY ROSENBAUM
& RUPERT VANDERVELL

Foreword by Andrew Marr

PERFECT PAIR PUBLISHING

First edition 2018

First published in Great Britain by Perfect Pair Publishing
35 Fitzroy Road, London NW1 8TP

ISBN: 978-1-9995844-0-5

Printed and bound in Wales by Gomer Press Ltd

All enquiries to danny@perfectpairpublishing.com
www.perfectpairpublishing.com

A catalogue record for this book is available from the British Library.

Contents

FOREWORD

ANDREW MARR

'A great city is first and foremost its people'

A great city isn't the buildings, though they help, or the parks, boulevards, grand squares, or even the cycle of weather. A great city is first and foremost its people, the characters whose hard work and zest bring those streets to life, and make life worth living in the middle of the thrum, chaos and noise for the rest of us. A great city is built up not from stones or glass, but from jokes, smiles and acts of random helpfulness. It derives its life from the sweat, persistence and professionalism of millions of people who the historians barely bother to notice.

Well, this book notices them. From barmen to beigel-bakers, fruiterers to art dealers, from those who care for rose-lovers in the parks to those who love dogs, from busy newspaper photographers to world-famous designers, dancers to bone-curators, it's a gloriously varied and often surprising portrait of modern London as it actually is. Most books about modern cities are, to put it politely, broad-brush – all photographic panoramas and heroic overstatements. This one, by contrast, is a form of reporterly pointillism: it is a composite portrait built up from tiny dabs of vivid colour, specific observations and local moments. It seems to me to get nearer to the truth about why contemporary London is such an enjoyable city for so many of us – not everyone – to live in.

So, global celebrities appear in passing, making a pilgrimage to Brick Lane for the very best of Jewish baking, or dropping into a Soho coffee bar for a perfect espresso. But they don't really dominate. Like most of us, they are passing through, mingling in the rich human confusion of 21st-century London. "Real Londoners" may indeed be able to trace their ancestry back for several estuarial generations. But

they may also have come here from deep France, Israeli cities, the United States or anywhere in Eastern Europe. London is said to have more major language groups than any other global capital; these sharply observed essays and beautiful photographs demonstrate it.

In the end, our contributions to a big city are really about what we do – the skills we bring, the hard work we put in, our agility, thoughtfulness, dexterity and ambition. So it's appropriate, in a service-economy metropolis, that so many of these stories are those of service or entertainment and the arts workers.

These are the people who feed us, entertain us, observe us and do their best to keep us sane. They work in some of the most famous places in the capital – the Dorchester hotel, Madame Tussauds, Regent's Park – and, in particular, adored, less-known nooks such as Bar Italia and Gordon's Wine Bar, an especially atmospheric slice of old London, surviving miraculously into these modern times.

There are, of course, notes of melancholy here. Old Battersea and old Soho, never mind Brick Lane, are gently surrendering to the commercialism of the modern world. It can sometimes seem as if idiosyncrasy and anything surprising have been bought up, homogenised and turned into bland chains by eager young venture capitalists. But, in fact, modern London still has plenty of captivating human surprises to offer if you look hard enough. Danny Rosenbaum and Rupert Vandervell have done exactly that; and by searching out the characters who make this city come alive, they have produced something much more interesting than a coffee table book.

INTRODUCTION

DANNY ROSENBAUM

'London is a roost for every bird'

Benjamin Disraeli

In August 2017, Rupert Vandervell and I came up with an idea: let's co-author a book using his photographs and my words, profiling 24 people who work in London, one for each hour of the day. It was a good idea, but we also got lucky. We found 24 remarkable people.

Coming from a background of making factual television, I am all too aware that thinking of a clever format is one thing but the quality of the show depends on what is called "the casting". The programmes live or die according to how engaging the people featured in them are. With *London Lives*, we have found 24 fascinating, often passionate characters.

It would be tempting to take all the credit for finding these individuals, but that would be disingenuous. Sometimes we did pinpoint the people we wanted. Perhaps we had seen a video of them, read an interview, or had some mutual connection and knew they would be eloquent and a suitable subject. Just as often, however, it was the individuals in PR and press departments who identified them for us.

In many cases, Rupert and I selected iconic places in London that we wanted to cover and it was with an open mind that we asked their press and PR departments to suggest who might be a willing and interesting person to profile. A large part of what made our research such fun has been dealing with not just the contributors but the people behind the scenes who brought them to us.

This book is about 24 individuals, the locations they work in and the jobs they do, but it is also a book about London. While researching these 24 wide-ranging stories it became obvious that some common themes were emerging. No matter

where they were born, nearly all of the people featured in this book consider themselves Londoners. Typical is Gerard Menan, the manager of Gordon's Wine Bar: "I'm a Londoner first, Frenchman second."

When we interviewed the midwife Freda Coker-Appiah, it emerged that University College London Hospital alone employs over 100 different nationalities. Paddington Bear was right: "The people of London are so various, they can all feel at home." *London Lives* organically developed into a celebration. We interviewed each person face-to-face and almost without exception they expressed their love for London.

The fruiterer Paul Murphy is a good example: "I've been all over the world. Yes, there are some other great cities, but for me nothing compares to London. All the different nationalities that are here now, it's fantastic. It has changed the food scene as well. When I came into the business 28 years ago, it was your Sunday roast vegetables and your oranges and your plums and pineapples. Now it's thousands of different products you could be asked for. It's a really good time to be in London and in food in London."

Nobody denies that the city has its problems. They are reported regularly in the media. However, the place to explore them is not *London Lives*. Instead, steered by the people we have profiled, we hope that the book is an uplifting and positive view of the capital city. Another hope is that the reader will be inspired by the passion displayed by the contributors and their lives. As you read through the book and the day starts to unfold, another common theme emerges. Whatever the time of day, the people we have featured enjoy their jobs and this

Statue of Benjamin Disraeli in Parliament Square

creates a virtuous circle of motivation leading to excellence to further motivation.

None of the people we have featured was born with a silver spoon in their mouth. Instead, they found their passion and worked hard to accomplish their achievements. Many had to overcome severe setbacks. For example, the Royal Ballet's Steven McRae suffered a serious injury early in his career which kept him off stage for a year. Some surgeons said that he would not dance again. However, he persevered and ended up progressing to the very top of his profession.

When does one day end and another begin? Rather than run our profiles from midnight onwards we wanted to create the feeling of the passing of a natural day. *London Lives* opens at 6am with the man in charge of Tower Bridge and ends at

5am in the maternity ward at University College Hospital, where each year around 6,600 new Londoners are welcomed into the world.

There is one element to the book that I have left until last because of its importance – the photography. Without fail, Rupert Vandervell's pictures have captured the essence of all the individuals. They are worth dwelling on as they illustrate the personalities and their characters on a different level from the text. Additionally, the images of their buildings' interiors and exteriors provide a striking tapestry of London. Each one evokes the time of day as well as the setting.

It has been an absolute joy researching and writing this book. It is my sincerest hope that the reader will experience a similar level of pleasure and satisfaction.

ACKNOWLEDGEMENTS

Firstly, we would like to thank the 24 people featured in this book. Not only did they give up their valuable time and sprinkle the book with insights and wisdom, but they also made the whole process of researching *London Lives* enjoyable.

Many thanks to Andrew Marr for taking the time to write the beautifully written foreword. You are an inspiration!

Thanks to all the following for their help in gaining access to the featured people and places: Naomi Ackerman, Kris Anwar, Alexandra Aspinall, Nick Biddle, John Chittenden, Alex Cowan, Callum Davies, Tor Evans, Lucy Fisher, Amy Hart, Ian Kenworthy, Sue Knowler, Aisling Lewis, Emily Parsons, Sophie Phillips, Simon Raw, Kelly Robinson, Lionel Roth, Ian Schofield, Piers Secunda, Nona Stancheva, Lucy Torchia, Elke Tullett, Alice Whitehead, Ashley Woodfield and Hannah Woolley.

We are also grateful to Izzie Thomas and Martin Rosenbaum, who provided valuable advice at crucial stages of the book. Thanks, too, to the team at our printers, Gomer Press, particularly Carys Hughes.

All the photographs are by Rupert, but we would like to thank Dr Johnson's House and the curator Celine Luppo McDaid for permission to take the photo at the house and for her co-operation and help with the launch.

It just remains for us to thank our families and friends for all the support they provided during the long period before this book saw the light of day. Additional thanks to Teresa Merrigan, who managed to catch errors and suggest improvements. If any mistakes slipped through the net, the fault lies with the authors.

Danny would like to dedicate *London Lives* to Sarah and reiterate that he loves her to bits!

CHRIS EARLIE

BRIDGE MASTER, TOWER BRIDGE

'People love the bridge. It's effectively a fairy-tale castle over a river'

Tower Bridge is quintessential London. Its beautiful façade is one of the city's most iconic images. As Chris Earlie, the man in charge, puts it: "People love the bridge. It's incredible the feedback we get on how much people love the structure. It is effectively a fairy-tale castle over a river." What is surprising to many is the wealth of activity that goes on behind the façade. It is now much more than a link across the Thames, lifting to allow boats through from early morning to late at night. Typical of London's regeneration, Tower Bridge has developed a first-division attraction out of its interior.

"We do everything nowadays: we open early for yoga sessions on top of our glass floor 42 metres above the Thames, we have autism-friendly mornings, we have family activity days, we have a dedicated learning programme, we're a filming location, an event venue, we have concerts down in the bascule chambers and we have an artist-in-residence programme," says Chris. As a result, the number of visitors has shot up to just under a million a year, and much of the growth has come from locals. Previously, 80% of visitors were from overseas whereas now it is nearer 60%.

Much of the success of Tower Bridge is down to the energy and enthusiasm of Chris, who grew up in Wales. He spent 10 years working in America before returning to the UK to do a master's degree at Cardiff School of Journalism, "which taught me I did not want to do journalism!".

Instead, in 2008, he became a marketing executive at Tower Bridge – a job that soon turned into a passion. "I didn't have much of a life outside work. I became fascinated with the bridge, fell in love with it. I spent all my weekends coming into work, spending time with the bridge master learning about the engineering and the operational side, even though my role was more about the promotion of the business."

Chris's unusual command of both the business and the engineering sides meant that four years ago he became the first person to combine the roles of head of bridge and bridge master. This is something of a juggling act. "A large part of my role is getting the balance right between the business imperatives and the obligation to the public, being custodian of the nation's icon, bearing in mind that we also have a statutory requirement to raise the bridge."

When Tower Bridge was completed in 1894, the area between it and London Bridge was the busiest trading port in the world. In the first year there were about 6,000 bridge lifts whereas now there are about 900 annually, mainly for tourist boats in the summer. It is a testimony to the great Victorian engineers who designed it that those lifts take as long today with an electric hydraulic system as they did back then, about eight minutes. The old system used steam engines, powered by huge coal boilers, to drive water under pressure to the lifting machinery. Anybody visiting the innards of the bridge can still see this amazingly impressive apparatus as well as the vast tanks acting as accumulators that were, in effect, Victorian rechargeable batteries. They contained enough power for a number of lifts, in case anything went wrong with the steam engines.

The bridge may have fewer vessels to contend with than in its early days, but the number of people crossing it has reached proportions unimaginable to the Victorians – about

There are about 900 bridge lifts annually, mainly for tourist boats in the summer

50,000 pedestrians, cyclists and motorists every day. One has to marvel at the complexity of Chris's job in the modern world: "The bridge is owned by the City of London Corporation, but it is not physically in the City; half of the bridge is in the borough of Southwark, half of it is in Tower Hamlets. In fact, since we had the walkways approved for weddings, there is actually a line marked on the bridge, so if you take a step over that line you are in the wrong borough and your nuptials are null and void!

"There are two police forces involved, the City of London police and the Met, and there are two river authorities, the Port Health Authority and the Port of London Authority. Historic England has a big part to play. Then there's also the Civil Aviation Authority, which had a big role in 2003 when the magician David Blaine was suspended beside the bridge. And, of course, there are various residents' groups. There's a lot of stakeholders. It's a big juggling act."

Chris is rightly proud of the developments at Tower Bridge, which have been accompanied by the regeneration of the area around it. But for all that, what has most impressed him is the change in Londoners themselves: "A big milestone was 2012, with the Olympics and also the Queen's Diamond Jubilee." The bridge displayed the Olympic rings during the event and had a starring role in the flotilla to mark the royal anniversary. "I have never known such a wonderful feeling of togetherness and shared experience," says Chris.

One of Tower Bridge's early morning lifts

JEREMY SELWYN

CHIEF PHOTOGRAPHER, EVENING STANDARD

'They made me doorstep an actor from EastEnders and he beat me up'

"Even at school I always wanted to be a photographer. I think I saw it as the easiest job in the world. All you do is use one finger to click a button." After a career spent taking photographs, Jeremy Selwyn is now the first to admit that it's hard work. In fact, it is his industry and professionalism as well as his creative talent that led to the Evening Standard's chief photographer being named National Newspaper Photographer of the Year in 2018.

Born in Edgware, northwest London, he moved to Hertfordshire and at school he went to see the careers advice officer. "I was told you mustn't even dream of being a photographer. I knew then that I would take it up – school and I didn't mix too well." College followed a similar pattern. "I was told by my head of department that he gave me the lowest pass ever because it would look bad for him if he gave me a fail."

Jeremy had, though, already started freelancing as a photographer, "skiving off" college to pursue his passion. His work started to appear in local papers, but he had his eye set on the nationals. "I went to every newspaper. I turned up in every newsroom because in those days you could just walk in. I took my portfolio, walked up to the picture desk. Eventually the Mail on Sunday gave me a bit of a trial, but then they said, no, go back to college, where I was officially at the time.

"So I used to turn up on news jobs that were happening and just do my own pictures. I got a breakthrough when a photo I took of Norman Tebbit pushing his wife in a wheelchair made the front page of the Daily Star. [The MP and his wife had been hurt in the Brighton bomb attack in 1984.] They then gave me shifts and for one of them they made me doorstep an actor from EastEnders. I was there one morning outside his house and he beat me up and smashed my cameras. I got a picture of him driving at me, trying to run me over, and that made the front page. The Star thought that was great and gave me a contract."

Jeremy stayed at the Star for a few years but when the deputy picture editor, David Ofield, moved to the Evening Standard to become picture editor he took Jeremy with him. "He was the greatest picture editor in the world, a legend in his own right, and without him I was nowhere," says Jeremy. That was February 1987 and Jeremy has been at the Standard ever since. "They have been very good to me. They've sent me everywhere I've wanted to go. I'm quite lucky, I get a free hand in a way. I do what they tell me to do, obviously – if there's a story breaking I'm sent on that by my picture editor, Elliot Wagland, but after years of working you have your own contacts and come up with your own stories and picture ideas. The Standard backs you to do those things."

One of Jeremy's main problems is the deadlines for the editions, because they are early in the day at roughly 10.30am and 12.30pm. He gets up at 4am and arrives in central London about an hour later. "I don't go into the office, there's no point, you can't take any pictures there. Any picture editor who sees his photographer sitting in the office knows he's doing nothing. Usually I get a call or email at 5am from the picture editor asking me to go somewhere or I might email him with a suggestion. Sometimes we do five jobs a day; news

'Sometimes we do five jobs a day; news in the mornings and features in the afternoons'

in the mornings and in the afternoons it tends to be features. It's a long day."

When Jeremy started at the Standard, now based in Kensington, there were 16 staff photographers. Today, it's just him. "I'm a chief photographer of one," he jokes. "At the moment I'm having a staff meeting!" According to Jeremy, you can't be shy or retiring as a news photographer. This makes sense when you meet him. Though he is highly affable and totally likeable, you can't help feeling there is a steel core inside him that ensures he gets the shot whatever the odds.

These days his rivals are not just other professional photographers but the general public, who can post pictures immediately on social media thanks to their smartphones. "My main form of competition is Twitter. If newspapers can use a photo from Twitter they will. If you beat Twitter and get your photo in first on a major news event, you've done well."

Over the years, Jeremy has photographed numerous politicians and royals. "Among my most memorable pictures are David Miliband holding a banana, Ed Miliband eating a bacon sandwich and, in a different vein, the Queen Mother looking up at the sky in the Field of Remembrance."

Possibly his favourite person to photograph is the Queen. "I love her, she's the best royal by a million miles. She's a professional. I did a portrait of her with the whole Cabinet when David Cameron was prime minister – it won royal picture of the year – and the Queen turned round to all the politicians and said, 'You are allowed to smile, you know.'"

Having spent three decades as the Evening Standard's chief photographer, Jeremy naturally is a great fan of London. "The river is my favourite place. I always do sunrises on the river when walking around in the morning. I've done 30 years of them."

Evening Standard stall at Oxford Circus station

JANE ANDERSON

COSTUME SUPERVISOR, MADAME TUSSAUDS

*'Captain America gets a hug
every now and then'*

Jane Anderson grew up just outside Glasgow and her passion for making clothes emerged at a very young age, when she would make tartan waistcoats and short trousers for her teddy bears while her grandmother tackled the kilts. At 20, she moved to London and initially sold merchandise for the indie band Senseless Things before working in the Psychedelic Supermarket in Kensington Market, making alterations to the clothes.

After a spell as a freelancer and for the theatrical costumier Monty Berman, Jane had a two-month stint at Madame Tussauds. She then worked for the Citizens Theatre in Glasgow, before deciding to return to London. While looking for fashion work, Jane took a job in a bar and in one those curious quirks of fate, where a chance happening changes the course of a life, her former supervisor at Madame Tussauds came in. Not only did she need a drink, she also needed a wardrobe assistant.

And so, in 2003, Jane started her second stint at Madame Tussauds. She became costume supervisor after just four months, and 15 years later she's still there. Although there are now more than 20 Madame Tussauds attractions around the world, London, which was the first, is very much the flagship. It attracts about 2 million visitors a year, who are all encouraged to get up close to the 300-plus waxworks, so it's no wonder the costumes require a lot of maintenance. "They can get very worn, particularly if people touch the same part of the costume. We do our best to maintain them to the highest standards," Jane says.

She and her team arrive at 7.30am and have a short period before the public enter in which to maintain the figures, brushing them down and doing sewing repairs. Unless there is major work needed, for example on the head, the figures are maintained in situ. To make the most of the time available, Jane and her team are adept at taking off the costumes and putting on the spares, which are prepared the day before, in less than half an hour. There are spare costumes for most of the figures. Marilyn Monroe's dress, for example, is usually changed weekly. "We have two dresses for Marilyn. We can shove them in the washing machine. They come out and they look beautiful and we don't even need to iron them."

After this busy maintenance session and a hearty breakfast, preparations are made for the following day: shirts ironed, costumes stained, cuffs attached securely. The rest of their time is filled with meetings and shopping for any items that are needed. Madame Tussauds regularly adds new people. Recent arrivals include Donald Trump and Tom Hardy. All the new figures are made painstakingly by hand and take on average three months to finish. Sometimes the subjects provide their own clothes. For example, Dame Helen Mirren donated an Asprey gown.

Jane's favourite group of figures is the French royal family, to whom she feels very attached. "I've grown with them. When I started at Madame Tussauds, Marie Antoinette's dress needed to be replaced. Then you also need to do the children and Louis XVI. It's a bit like painting the Sydney Harbour Bridge: you get them all done and then you have to start all over again." Apart from the French royals, Jane has a soft spot for the Marvel Super Hero figures. "Captain America gets a hug every now and then." So seamless (pun intended) is the Madame Tussauds experience that the multitude of visitors would be amazed at the amount of hard work and attention to detail that goes on behind the scenes.

Donald Trump is one of more than 300
wax figures at Madame Tussauds

TOM MOSS-DAVIES

HEAD GARDENER, REGENT'S PARK

'I'm a working foreman, not somebody who walks around with a clipboard'

When you first meet Tom Moss-Davies you are instantly aware that you are in the company of one of life's characters. For a start, more likely than not he will be wearing a deerstalker hat – appropriate for a man who has spent more than four decades of his career just a short walk from 221b Baker Street, the home of Sherlock Holmes.

This year, Tom retires from his role as head gardener of Regent's Park, including the beautiful Queen Mary's Gardens (QMG), where 17,000 rose bushes bloom in summer. This beautiful and fragrant corner of the capital is a far cry from Tom's early days playing on the bombsites of London's East End. His childhood was spent in Bethnal Green, Shoreditch and also Islington, all areas that have been transformed since Tom was a boy. Now trendy, they were rundown when he grew up.

After leaving school, Tom had various engineering jobs, but was already fed up with working in a building with no windows or access to sunlight when he had an accident at work which left him fearful of machinery. So, at the suggestion of his brother-in-law, he took a job as an assistant gardener at Regent's Park in 1973. "I never looked back," says Tom. Not that it was easy. "I had a hard boss but he had a foreman who taught me how to do everything with a spade, and I mean everything: dig it over, dead flat, right height and the right till, never use a rake. If you got caught with a rake, you'd know about it. He was hard. Old school."

Tom gradually moved up the grades before being appointed foreman of Queen Mary's Gardens in 1985. "I've changed a lot of QMG – built great big rockeries on islands using 2½ tons of rock, remodelled the big waterfall, revamped the shape of loads of beds." QMG houses London's largest collection of roses. It was named after the wife of King George V and opened to the public in 1932. These days it boasts 84 immaculately turned out beds with between 90 and 210 roses in each (pictured overleaf). The best blooms are usually to be seen in early June. The summer display runs from May until September and winter bedding from October to May. Regent's Park takes about half of all the bedding plants grown for the eight royal parks in London.

Tom gets up at 5am for a 7am start at work and finishes around 3.30pm. "I'm a working foreman, not somebody who walks around with a clipboard. I'm hands-on and lead by example. People like that. Respect is not given to you like a little monument, you have to earn it." By way of example, Tom, who works all over the park not just on QMG, this year spent two weeks wielding a chainsaw as part of preparations for the winter garden.

Visitors come from all over the world to admire the roses. In summer, the park is so full of people that Tom likens it to a beehive. That said, much of the time there is a tranquillity that Tom appreciates as a welcome contrast to the hustle and bustle of London. Since 1996 he has lived in Hertfordshire, where, as a keen astronomer, he has built his own observatory.

There's no doubt that the beauty of Regent's Park owes a lot to Tom's rare mix of great industry and inspired creativity. "I've worked in Regent's Park for 45 years. I've put quite a lot of my life into this job, I've liked it and it's given me a lot of pleasure."

ALI TAYLOR

HEAD OF CANINE BEHAVIOUR,
BATTERSEA DOGS & CATS HOME

'I'm like a stick of rock, I have Battersea written inside me'

Ali Taylor may have been born in Harlesden, north London, but as she says: "I am like a stick of rock – if you cut me in half, I have Battersea written inside me." Ali has been at Battersea Dogs & Cats Home for 25 years and is now head of canine behaviour and training. Her life revolves around dogs, not just at work but at home too. She has fostered more than 500, taking them in and looking after them until they find a permanent home. Ali jokes that she has had five "failures" at fostering, by which she means five dogs that she decided to keep.

It is a far cry from her early childhood, when dogs weren't allowed in the house because her mother was petrified of them. The very day her parents separated, when Ali was 10 years old, her father bought her a puppy. These days, Ali's mother still has problems with the likes of chihuahuas but adores one of her daughter's dogs, a Staffordshire bull terrier called Squirt.

Ali Taylor's life around dogs might have been very different. Having enjoyed a spell travelling around the world in her youth, she got back to London and wanted to earn some money quickly to go travelling again. She applied for jobs at just three places: Miss Selfridge, HMV and Battersea. Fate decreed that it would be Battersea that offered her the job.

When she started, Ali was a kennel hand, mainly cleaning out the dogs' enclosures. It was supposed to be just a short-term job, but, as Ali puts it: "From the day I started until now I feel exactly the same – I've never looked at the clock. The job just took over." Now she manages a team of 20 people across three sites. In addition to the southwest London headquarters there

are rescue centres at Windsor and Brands Hatch. At any one time, Battersea houses about 150 dogs and 140 cats. It takes in strays via local councils and accepts animals from people who can no longer look after them.

The reasons dogs come in vary from the bizarre to the tragic. Ali recalls a case where an owner brought one in "because it no longer matched the carpet", while other owners have found they don't have long to live or have become homeless. Often, Battersea doesn't know an animal's history. When information is available, it can be hard to believe. For example, recently a dog called Sparkles was left to die in a suitcase, and couldn't walk when he arrived. Fortunately, he proved a success story, as he not only survived but was trained and found a good home.

Not all the training is for dogs; much of it is for people. Battersea offers behavioural consultations for customers, education for the community generally and for specific groups such as young offenders. As well as the 437 staff there are about 1,000 volunteers, up from only about 20 when Ali started in the 1990s.

Battersea has come a long way since its foundation in 1860 by Mary Tealby as the Temporary Home for Lost and Starving Dogs. In 1871 it moved from Holloway in north London to its current site, which has been expanded and upgraded. The exterior is striking with its nest of modern buildings sitting next to the iconic Battersea Power Station. The interiors are bright and cheerful with classical music permeating through the kennels, calming the latest intake of animals.

While Battersea is an undoubted success, Ali worries about what lies ahead for pets in London because of the rules

The reasons dogs come in to Battersea can vary from the bizarre to the tragic

of councils and housing associations: "A lot of dogs come to us when people are moving and are not allowed to have a dog in the new property, and now there are a lot of places where they are not allowed. There are more and more rules and regulations and there may come a time, in 10 or 15 years, when people think it's not worth having a dog."

She points out the positives of keeping a four-legged friend and explains that different people expect very different things from a dog: "Battersea is like a dating agency – we need to find out what it is the person wants from their pet. Some people want a dog to sit quietly next to them watching Coronation Street, others want an active dog bouncing around. Our job is about matching up the owner and the dog. There's no point giving someone who's not active a dog that's very lively. It's not going to be a marriage made in heaven – a little bit like my mum and dad."

As for herself: "I like people and I like dogs, I'm in the right job." Ali Taylor and Battersea Dogs & Cats Home – definitely a match made in heaven.

At any one time Battersea houses about 150 dogs

10.30am
A peaceful haven in the heart of London,
Berkeley Square Gardens dates back to
the 18th century. Winston Churchill lived
at number 48 as a child

Dr ANDREA TANNER

ARCHIVIST, FORTNUM & MASON

'I'm regularly on eBay and other sites buying back bits of our heritage'

Flanagan & Allen, Lennon & McCartney, Morecambe & Wise step aside, there is nothing more quintessentially English than Fortnum & Mason. The upmarket department store's archivist, Andrea Tanner, may hail from Glasgow but it would be hard to find anyone more immersed in London history. After leaving Scotland at the age of 20 to study for a master's degree at Warwick University she came to the capital to write her dissertation. It was supposed to be just a three-month stay, but she never went back north. Instead, Andrea took on a variety of interesting roles, working at the Public Record Office, as a genealogist at the College of Arms and as an assistant archivist at Great Ormond Street Hospital.

It was in 1996 that she joined Fortnum & Mason, and she remains a vibrant force there today. It is hard to imagine anybody more effusive about London, Fortnum's and the role of the archivist. According to Andrea: "The archivist is the keeper of the company memory. Because we're normally shy and retiring, people forget it's the archivists who decide what is remembered. If we don't hang on to something, people won't remember it."

Fortnum's was founded over 300 years ago in 1707, coincidentally the same year Britain was formed when Scotland joined England and Wales. The store has always been on the same site in Piccadilly. Unfortunately, however, lots of its records have not survived. "Shops are a bit like theatres – it's the next production that is the most important," says Andrea. Also, before her, there was no one tasked with the responsibility of systematically preserving Fortnum's heritage.

"What survived before I came on board survived by

happenstance. One of my jobs is to dig out old stories so I spend a lot of my time in other archives, hoovering up what they've got. I'm regularly on eBay and other websites buying back bits of our heritage. Caviar pots and wicker baskets are the items that most often come up for auction. Nowadays, our buyers and the shopfloor staff know that before they throw anything out, they've got to tell Dr T!"

One of the oldest items in Andrea's collection is a catalogue from 1843, but the most prized object she has found is Shackleton's original order for his Antarctic expedition in 1914. It was not unusual for Fortnum's to supply expeditions. Mallory and Irvine's 1924 ascent of Everest was another notable order, and customers would often request provisions for trips such as tiger hunts in Borneo. "Sending things around Britain, in fact to the rest of the world, is in our DNA because we have been doing it from the very beginning. Sending perishable goods across the globe is in our character," says Andrea.

Legend has it that Fortnum's started by selling candles. However, its most important product became tea – 200 varieties in all! "It was a hugely important commodity in the 18th and 19th centuries. Very expensive, easily adulterated, so people came to Fortnum's for its provenance," she says. "Fortnum's catered for the landed gentry, the upper-middle classes and the aristocracy. We engaged a lady, Miss Joyce Wethered, who was the British women's golfing champion and she would sell you clubs made to her specification. We had a miniature putting green in the store so she could help you.

"We engaged Commander GW Hillyard, who was the secretary of the All England Club, and he would sell you

Two of Fortnum's teas are grown in Britain – one in Cornwall, one in Scotland

rackets and tennis whites and organise to have your tennis court laid, indoors or outdoors. In the winter we hired a great skier, Vivian Caulfeild. He would sell you shoes made specifically for Fortnum's and we had a miniature ski slope on which you could have a little practice on your wooden skis."

Unlike most archive jobs, much of Andrea's work is "front-facing". She looks after VIPs, takes members of the public on tours of the building and speaks to new staff as part of their induction. On the first, second and third floors, 70% of what the store sells is of British manufacture. On the ground floor, it is different because only two of the 200 teas it stocks are grown in Britain – one in Cornwall, one in Scotland. That said, all the tea is blended in England and all the biscuits and jams are made in Britain.

Fortnum's has a difficult balancing act: on the one hand it wants to provide a comforting continuity, but it also wants to be a trendsetter. "You don't get to be 311 years old by staying the same, you have to keep evolving to keep your current customers and attract new ones," says Andrea.

Its philosophy is to give people pleasure. "We want people to think about Fortnum's and smile." Talking of which, if you have ever wondered who writes the jokes in the store's Christmas crackers, that's another string to Andrea's bow.

Any final thoughts on London? "I love this city. I like getting out of it, but I like coming back because I'm coming home. I'm not going to leave London – my plot at the Brompton Cemetery is waiting!"

Fortnum's biggest-selling item is its Royal Blend tea – one of 200 varieties

KARL STANDLEY

HEAD GROUNDSMAN, WEMBLEY STADIUM

'I had a tear in my eye. I looked at the pitch and thought, wow, we made it happen'

Karl Standley has an infectious enthusiasm. He loves stadiums and he loves horticulture. Not surprising, then, that he jumped at the chance to join the ground staff at Wembley Stadium when he first heard about the opportunity. Born in Fair Oak, a farming village near Southampton, his passion was already apparent when for his GCSE in IT he designed a computer program that provided information on football stadiums around the world.

After leaving school he joined the ground staff at Southampton FC. Four years later, in 2006, he heard about a job at Wembley and became a junior groundsman there. When he arrived, the new Wembley Stadium was still a construction site: "It took my breath away. My first thought was how big it was. It was a monstrosity. My second thought was how are we going to grow grass in this stadium. We now know how to, but in the early days we didn't." Karl progressed up the ranks. "When I got the role of head groundsman in 2015 it was my proudest day. It was a dream. I wear my heart on my sleeve and I'm very proud of what I do. It's not just work – I'm proud of my home life, and of my team at Wembley."

Karl is quick to emphasise the importance of his staff and he has aphorisms displayed around the office, such as "There is no I in Wembley, but there is a We" and "Alone you can go fast, together you can go far". The achievements of his team's 2017-18 season were extraordinary. Nobody has ever managed to put on that level of activity before. Covering Tottenham Hotspur's home games on top of all Wembley Stadium's other activities presented a huge challenge, but Karl believes in making the impossible possible. From August to May, a

Premier League team with a decent Cup run would expect to have about 35 home games. Karl and his team surpassed that in just four months.

The full 12 months saw the pitch in use about 70 times. As well as the Spurs games, there were NFL games, the Emirates FA Cup semi-finals and final, home games for the England national team, rugby league and rugby union fixtures, a corporate hospitality pitch day and training sessions. There were also pop concerts by the likes of Adele.

Each event brings its own challenges, such as repairing the turf after the colossal weight of the stage for a concert. Most ground staff have seven weeks to get a pitch ready for a season; Karl and his team had less than a month after the Adele shows. He says: "We have to artificially grow the pitch. We use large lamps of high-pressure sodium bulbs that are like fake sunlight. At three in the morning, when we are all sleeping, the pitch is still growing. We're artificially speeding up the process.

"There are certain things I can't control, for example, the weather. We try to cater for all eventualities but when it comes to the old man in the sky he's the boss. Wembley Stadium has a very difficult microclimate; in the winter it's a fridge, in the summer it's an oven. We have a system underneath the pitch, where we can blow air into it and make it act like a lung. We can also pull air through the pitch, and moisture, and make the pitch drain quicker."

The grass is the most protected thing in the stadium. It is patrolled by a security guard at night and there is a 24-hour camera observing it. There are three small cubes on the pitch

that send updates to Karl every minute, including information on humidity, soil moisture and temperature. "When I wake up at 5.30am, the first thing I'll do is say good morning to my wife and then I'll look at the system and be able to plan for the day. The pitch is special, I call it a 'she', our little girl." However, it's not just about technology. Karl and his colleagues constantly inspect the pitch, and use old-fashioned lawnmowers and tractors. Also, they use string to help them paint the lines and to ensure the mowing and cutting produce as immaculate a surface as possible. There is a family of kestrels living in the roof of the stadium which are useful for keeping away the pigeons and crows.

Being a groundsman is not just about growing grass; there's a commercial side as well. Karl's job is about enabling as many events to happen as possible without sacrificing the quality of the pitch. He is involved in planning many years ahead, liaising with the scheduling and events teams. His bosses keep telling him to take time off, but he says: "The grass is always growing and I have to continually manage that. It's not a 9-5 job. I chose this career and I have only myself to blame, but I love it." On those rare days when Karl does find himself with free time, he loves just walking around London, exploring new areas. "It's a magnificent city and it still amazes me. It is so diverse and vibrant."

For Karl, the 2017-18 season was an amazing learning curve, and showed the strength of his team. Even before that, though, there were many proud moments. He recalls the end of the previous season: "We had a busy schedule, we had long hours, lots of out-of-the-box thinking, and it was England v Malta and the anthem was about to be played. I've always sung it, and I remember the last verse I cracked up on. I had a tear in my eye. I looked at the pitch and thought, wow, we made it happen."

Lamps with high-pressure sodium bulbs help the grass grow at Wembley Stadium

43

1.14pm
Office workers spill out onto Reuters
Plaza at Canary Wharf for a quick lunch

RICHARD BARFOOT

PROPRIETOR, SWEETINGS RESTAURANT

'He gets the final word – he is God'

The City of London has gone through a multitude of changes since Sweetings moved to its current building in 1890, but anyone who dined at 39 Queen Victoria Street well over a century ago would recognise the same fish and oyster restaurant today.

One early customer was the painter Henri de Toulouse-Lautrec. Sweetings was his favourite restaurant in London and he wrote to his mother applauding its skate wings in black butter. The grade II-listed building is located on a triangular corner site (think the Flatiron Building in New York) in the heart of the City. The oak panelling, mosaic floors and high ceilings immediately fill visitors with nostalgia when they enter what is one of London's oldest restaurants.

Since 2000, this City institution has been owned by Richard (Dick) Barfoot and his philosophy has been to change as little as possible. The bill of fare, as the menu is termed, has been largely the same for decades, so too the interior, apart from no longer having sawdust floors, and many of the staff have been there almost as long, or longer, than the proprietor himself.

Dick was born in Sunderland in 1936 and came to London when he was five years old. He left school at 15 to join the fishmonger chain Mac Fisheries and has worked in the same business ever since. In 1980 he created his own supplier company, Barfoot (London) Ltd, which still thrives. Sweetings was previously owned by his friend Graham Needham, who had been a chef at the Mayfair fish restaurant Scott's. Dick's eyes light up as he recounts how, when Graham's widow asked if he might be interested in buying the business from her, he took up her offer "with both hands".

Dick had been a customer of Sweetings since the 1970s. Other notable diners past and present include the actors Larry Hagman, Keira Knightley and Gwendoline Christie, the singer Grace Jones, chefs such as Jamie Oliver, Rick Stein and Fergus Henderson (who proposed to his wife Margot there), and characters such as the furrier Mr Prager, who was still a regular at the restaurant in his nineties.

A lot of the clientele are regulars. A striking example is the man, who shall remain anonymous, who got rather drunk one day many years ago and bought a signed cricket bat at a charity auction for a small fortune. He felt unable to go home to his wife with it and so the bat has hung on the wall of the restaurant to this day.

There is a community spirit about the place. It takes no reservations and customers are seated on a first come, first served basis. The early sitting is around noon and tends to be quick. Those in search of a more leisurely lunch come in at about 1.30pm with no set end time.

This atmosphere of camaraderie is clear among the staff. Their nationalities are diverse, including French, Polish, Albanian and Ghanaian – and Spanish, in the case of head waiter Angelo, who has worked at Sweetings for over 30 years. They all seem equally at home here in the heart of London's financial district. Every Friday, after the second service is finished, the staff sit down to fish and chips, accompanied by wine.

Crucial to the smooth running of the restaurant is the manager, Alison Perrott. She has been at Sweetings for more than 15 years, starting as cashier. She was born and grew up

The interior has changed little for decades apart from no longer having sawdust floors

in Hertfordshire but now lives on the Sussex coast and each morning takes the 7.30am train to London. She met her Nigerian husband while working at the jazz club Ronnie Scott's. Alison handles the day-to-day running of the restaurant, dealing with all manner of tasks such as accounts and stock control. She's also in charge of front-of-house duties, and has developed a sort of sign language with the waiting staff to get her message across discreetly. For example, walking past a waiter with two fingers pressed subtly against her cheek indicates that she needs a table for two as soon as possible.

Also, in a rare example of modernity at Sweetings, she has used Google Translate to understand the requirements of three Chinese teenagers, who ended up very happy with their seafood and colas. They were a relatively unusual group of diners, but tourists do come in numbers because of the restaurant's reputation and its proximity to the likes of Tate Modern, the Globe theatre and the Tower of London.

Though Alison makes the day-to-day decisions, all the major matters are referred to Dick. As she puts it: "He gets the final word – he is God."

Sweetings takes no reservations and customers
are seated on a first come, first served basis

ZANDRA RHODES

FASHION DESIGNER AND FOUNDER
OF THE FASHION AND TEXTILE MUSEUM

'In 1977 people called me the Princess of Punk'

To be at the top of your profession for half a century takes some doing in any field but it is an extraordinary feat in such a shifting landscape as the fashion industry. However, Dame Zandra Rhodes is a human dynamo, and her propensity to work and stay passionate about design has seen her stamp her mark on the fashion world for more than five decades.

Born in Chatham, Kent, in 1940, Zandra came to London when she was 21 to study printed textile design at the Royal College of Art. She found it quite hard to adjust to the city at first. "I was quite boring and missed living at home. I might go to college dances on a Friday or Saturday evening but apart from that I was always working."

Her boyfriend at the time, Alex MacIntyre, ran the bar at the dances. "When we graduated, the college asked us to wear black but I wore a white suit printed with huge black spots and black-and-white brogue shoes. Sadly, I don't have a picture. What's more, Alex took all my old clothes, including that outfit, to Oxfam without me knowing. He would say that our flat was too full of my clothes. I had to buy some of them back."

Zandra spent the early Sixties in London. "It felt it was a swinging, happening place, if only in our minds. Fashion wise, you had Mary Quant, the Vidal Sassoon haircuts, and Grace Coddington was modelling in the Royal College shows."

She showed her printed textiles to the Italian fashion designer Emilio Pucci, who turned her down for a job and said she should design in black and white. Zandra taught at Ravensbourne College of Art and also in High Wycombe to make ends meet. Then she had her first big breakthrough making prints for two young designers, Foale and Tuffin, in Carnaby Street. After a few years, in a typical-for-Zandra blend of a search for creative freedom and a desire for commercial success, she set up her own business. She went into partnership with Sylvia Ayton and with backing from the actress Vanessa Redgrave opened The Fulham Road Clothes Shop. Her work was becoming successful, David Bailey was photographing her dresses, but her career really took off in 1969 when she crossed the Atlantic and her work was featured in American Vogue.

In the early 1970s the fashion mogul Ronnie Sterling backed Zandra in her own shop just off Bond Street and by the end of the decade her prominence in London's fashion world was assured. "In 1977 I did the punk collection and people called me the Princess of Punk. It didn't sell well, but it helped make my name." Then, as now, the fabrics were screenprinted. "Everything you see of mine is still hand silkscreen printed. We are probably the only people to still screen print in London."

Her time nowadays is divided between London and the USA, which is the home of her partner Salah Hassanein, who was a senior executive in the entertainment industry.

In London, she lives and works at her studio in Bermondsey, attached to the Fashion and Textile Museum, which she founded. When her friend Andrew Logan pointed out the building to her in the 1990s, Bermondsey was regarded as a down-and-out area, but like so much of London it has been regenerated and is now trendy.

The museum building echoes the wider area. Previously

Zandra's vision has given the museum a strikingly colourful exterior

it was drab and grey, but Zandra's vision, further developed by the Mexican architect Ricardo Legorreta, has resulted in a strikingly colourful exterior with a spacious, bright feel inside. The museum was opened by Princess Michael of Kent in 2003.

These days Zandra – a self-proclaimed workaholic – is as busy as ever. Recently she finished her rug collection, designed prints for Valentino and 48 flags to hang around the Southbank Centre during the B(old) festival, which celebrated the lives of people over 65. She is an early morning person. "I start work around 7am. I don't take lunch – I might grab a snack, but, I hate going out to lunch, it always puts me in a bad mood."

She is also a great believer in persistence. "For design ideas you have to work at things. Sometimes it seems like it's not working, but the light comes at the end of the tunnel."

Zandra has dressed numerous celebrities, including Diana, Princess of Wales ("she was very shy and bit her nails") and the singers Diana Ross and Kylie Minogue. It's not the fame that appeals. "I find every project interesting. In fact, when Freddie Mercury came to me for a top, I didn't even know what music Queen played. Afterwards, I went to one of Queen's concerts and felt like I was a middle-aged freak."

In fact, Dame Zandra is an enchanting woman, friendly and open, with a ready smile. Her face lights up when she talks of tending her beautiful terrace garden or entertaining friends for dinner. She is a fan of London and while she claims not to go out enough – "I tend to be a bit of a hermit" – she loves evenings at the V&A and the Tate. It is great to see that after five decades of wonderful creativity, her passion burns as brightly as ever.

The Fashion and Textile Museum
in Bermondsey

MOHAMMED ANZAOUI

CLUB STEWARD,
THE REFORM CLUB

*'I love the club.
It has a soul and a spirit'*

Walk up the steps of the imposing Reform Club at 104 Pall Mall, and one of the first people you are likely to meet is Mohammed Anzaoui, club steward. A tall, elegant man, Mohammed often greets members and their guests as they make their way into the historic club, in the heart of London. It is a far cry from the small Moroccan town, just outside Tangier, where he was born.

After growing up in Morocco, Mohammed followed his father to Gibraltar, where he got a taste of British culture and decided to move to London in 1989 to carve out a life here. He recalls his surprise when he first arrived: "Gibraltar is just a rock; it was a shock coming to London – a giant town. I didn't know anyone. It was hard at first. The first place I worked at was a factory in Wembley. Everyone else was Indian. They didn't speak English. After one year I wondered if I'd made a mistake. But then I moved to central London and got a job at Le Méridien hotel."

Not long after, he started work at the Royal Over-Seas League, where one of his highlights was meeting the Queen. After a year, he heard about an opening for the assistant chamberlain role at the Reform. Like many of us, he did not even know what it meant at first. The Oxford dictionary gives the definition from Middle English as a servant in a bedchamber. Initially Mohammed was a tea boy for those staying at the club. It was the start of a long career at the Reform in a variety of roles. But Mohammed recalls when he was interviewed for his first role there in 1991 by the then secretary. "I still remember. He said, 'I don't think the club is ready for a Mohammed,' so I said, 'Well, you can call

me what you like, as long as you give me the job.'" Times have changed, and members now refer to him not just by his nickname, Pinto, but also as Mo or even Mohammed. In his time at the club, Mohammed has been a casual in the kitchen, a barman, the front hall night porter, but has held his current position of club steward since 2008.

One of his more unusual roles was, in effect, being a carer. He used to look after the Reform Club member Geoffrey Hartog, the last full-time resident, who lived in the accommodation there for over 40 years. Hartog used to wear a bowler hat and walk around the club in his slippers. When he became ill with cancer, he did not want a nurse but asked for someone from the club to look after him, and so it was that Pinto, as well as his weekday job, spent his weekends caring for Hartog and taking him to synagogue.

In those days, Hartog paid just £40 a month for accommodation. Nowadays members are not allowed to stay for extended periods but short-term accommodation is available for around £150 a night. Times have also changed for the staff. They no longer stay in the club, but Mohammed recalls that he lived at the Reform from 1991-1995. Like a lot of the staff, he stayed in the third-floor rooms. His enthusiasm for the Reform is infectious. "I love the club. It has a soul and a spirit."

While working there he has met Princess Anne, Mikhail Gorbachev and Margaret Thatcher. They came as guests or speakers at the numerous functions, but the club boasts many famous former members, including past prime ministers Churchill, Gladstone, Lloyd George and

Asquith. The latter even held ministerial meetings in the secret Cabinet Room, accessed by a hidden door from the beautiful dining room, called the Coffee Room, which paradoxically used to be the only room where you were not allowed to be served coffee.

After leaving the club's accommodation, Mohammed moved to Elephant & Castle and then to Kennington. He and his second wife, also from Morocco, have two daughters who were born in Guy's Hospital. His wife teaches Arabic.

Mohammed tends to work from 11am to 8.30pm. "My relationship with the members has always been friendly. I am the bridge between them and the secretary. If they have concerns they like to see Pinto. I have always done my best for the members. I'm always lurking around, checking everything is in order, that everyone is escorted to the room they want. I keep tabs on where everyone is, every person within the club is accounted for. I'm looking at every angle of the club, looking at every corner – I'm a little bit nosey. The club has been good to me and I have always been good to it. I count myself as an asset to the club."

The Saloon at the Reform Club

57

The Smoking Room, originally known as
the Upper Library, at the Reform Club

Dr HEATHER BONNEY

PRINCIPAL CURATOR, HUMAN REMAINS AND ANTHROPOLOGY,
NATURAL HISTORY MUSEUM

'I wanted to be a doctor but wasn't really a people person – the dead ones don't talk back!'

Visitors to the absorbing and extensive Natural History Museum might be surprised that the exhibits are just one element of a vast operation. The museum employs around 850 people, of which 300 are scientists working behind the scenes. Dr Heather Bonney, the principal curator of human remains and anthropology, is one of them. Born in Wokingham, Berkshire, she used to come into London to visit the museum as a child.

Heather decided while still young to be a forensic pathologist. "I wanted to do medicine and be a doctor but I wasn't really a people person, and the dead ones don't talk back!" In fact, Heather is personable and displays a cheerful personality in spite of, or perhaps because of, spending a lot of her time around skulls and skeletons.

In the last year of her degree in forensic science, she was involved in the excavation of Anglo Saxon burial sites that had been discovered in the basement of a house in Lincoln. They contained the skeletal remains of about 80 people. "Just from looking at the bones we could tell how old they were, whether they were male or female, how tall they were, sometimes what their ancestry was, and what diseases they might have had, such as osteoarthritis, some cancers and tuberculosis," says Heather.

She went on to do a master's degree at Sheffield in human osteology and funerary archaeology (the archaeology of burials and the social aspects of how people were buried and why), then returned to Lincoln to do a PhD in forensic anthropology. In 2008 she joined the Natural History Museum, where many of the staff are, like her, long servers. "There is continuity. It's not just a public-facing museum, it's also a scientific institution with a lot of research going on into subjects such as climate change, parasitic disease and human evolution."

Heather is responsible for the collections in the anthropology section, which encompass not just the remains of 25,000 people but numerous artefacts and fossil primates. The amount of human remains on view to the public is deliberately limited. "We only display remains in the human evolution gallery if they are demonstrating a fundamental scientific point that can't be demonstrated with replicas," says the curator

"It is important for people to see real remains in galleries, rather than casts all the time, so we do have a human skeleton in the human evolution gallery to compare with other fossils and other primates. The vast majority, though, are used for research, which can be forensic, medical or archaeological, looking at past populations, human health and disease."

The museum's collection of human remains found in London includes 740 individuals who lived in the city over the past 5,000 years. They were mostly uncovered during big construction projects, such as under the MI5 headquarters, Waterloo station and the Lloyd's insurance building.

The remains of about 130 people came from the River Thames. "They are an enigma," says Heather. "When you excavate a burial from under a building you have clues such as associated artefacts and dating clues from the soil, but the remains in the Thames have no context. The interesting thing is that they were largely skulls and there is a debate whether they were deposited there deliberately or washed there from

The museum employs about 850 people, of which 300 are scientists working behind the scenes

cemeteries through tributaries. The latter is possible because skulls would roll but the rest of the body would not." The skulls come from different periods, from prehistoric through Roman to post-mediaeval.

Heather observes about her feelings when working with human remains: "It's not purely scientific. You can get quite attached to individuals that you are working on over a long period. It's not eerie or weird, but you can feel sad about things that have happened to people when you work out their story. You can feel awestruck and you can definitely feel a connection to them."

As well as working at one, Heather also enjoys visiting museums. "One of the great changes since I've lived in London is the number of evening events and talks when the galleries are closed, where you can enjoy experiences and interact more with ideas. To engage the public with science is a great thing." There can be no doubt that the Natural History Museum and Dr Heather Bonney are themselves doing that in fine fashion.

The anatomical miracle of the giraffe on display in the Natural History Museum's Hintze Hall

4.55pm
The sun sets over London,
viewed from the Royal Observatory
in Greenwich Park

THE VERY REVEREND DAVID ISON

DEAN OF ST PAUL'S CATHEDRAL

'I'm just a parish priest, yet I'm responsible for running a £10m business'

David Ison seems to be a man who likes a challenge. Throughout his career he has been pitched into demanding roles. However, David is not a firefighter; he is someone who has a vision and takes a long-term view of the jobs he accepts. He was born in Brentwood, Essex, in 1954 to parents who met in a church youth group and married in South Woodford, where his grandfather was a vicar. As a child, he used to stand on Brentwood High Street, which is at the top of a hill, and look 20 miles along the Roman Road to the dome of St Paul's Cathedral in the far distance. "But I never thought I'd have anything to do with it."

After university and theological college, David and his wife felt called to go to the inner city and from 1979 to 1988 he worked in Deptford and Greenwich, southeast London. "I was there during the Thatcher years. I marched on the streets against some of the policies of the government at the time." Decades later, as Dean of St Paul's, David oversaw Margaret Thatcher's funeral.

His next challenge was as a vicar in Potters Green, Coventry, where the church was in a sorry state. "It needed rebuilding physically and spiritually and reconnecting with the community," David recalls. He moved on to Exeter, where he had his first experience of working in a cathedral, and then, in 2005, he was appointed Dean of Bradford, which had been the country's first bankrupt cathedral. Six years on, having turned around the fortunes of Bradford, David was approached about becoming Dean of St Paul's. Initially, he did not jump at the opportunity. "Two days before Christmas in 2011, I was about to go on sabbatical for three months and they said

they wanted me to apply. I said, 'I don't want to … I know nothing about St Paul's, it's for posh people and I've always gone to inner cities and difficult areas.' They persisted – 'The Church wants you to apply.' So I said, 'Well, the interviews are when I'll be in Tiberius in Israel, on sabbatical with my wife, so I can't come. Sorry about that.' And then they said, 'We will pay for you to fly back', and I realised, knowing the Church of England, I was in deep do-do at that point!"

At the interview, David made clear: "If you want someone to put St Paul's back together again [after the Occupy London protest] the answer is no. But if you want someone to answer the question, 'What does God want this cathedral to be in the 21st century and how do we get there', that's the kind of thing that would interest me." Sure enough, he was offered the job and was thrown in at the deep end. "I had been at St Paul's 10 days when the Queen turned up with 56 members of her family for her Diamond Jubilee, which was beyond terrifying You think, well, it's just a grandma coming to church. It's a family, let's welcome them like you would any family."

Although the Occupy London camp had gone before David's arrival, there were still rumblings and on the anniversary of the anti-capitalism protest four women chained themselves to the pulpit. "I said, 'I think I can honestly say this is the first time I've had a truly captive audience.' I met them afterwards and we ended up doing a demonstration together on Parliament Square, drawing attention to the plight of people with disabilities."

On a normal day, David gets to the cathedral at 7.15am for morning prayer, then from 8.30am he will be engaged in

events and administration. At 5pm there is evensong and after that there may be dinners, meetings or tasks such as writing sermons and dealing with correspondence. "It's one of the curious things; I'm just a parish priest and yet I'm responsible for the running of a £10 million business."

In the morning, the clergy make up the core of those in attendance and at evensong it is mainly visitors. There are around 200 regular worshippers. It is not a congregation in the normal sense; for example, there is not a parish hall. David explains: "Technically speaking I'm the dean of the smallest cathedral city in the country because the City of London has only about 8,000 residents." While he accepts that London has problems – there is greater inequality and more individualism than elsewhere, rather than a sense of community – he is positive about the capital. "People are no less caring than they were and there is a sense of diversity that I love. There is a huge variety of cultures, which enriches life for everyone. It is believed to be the most diverse city on the planet ever."

He sees one of his main tasks as making St Paul's as inclusive as possible, not just for people of different cultural backgrounds, but also those with disabilities and different sexualities. "We want to be a place anyone can come to. For example, we say to groups of children from Bangladeshi schools in the East End, if you're British this is part of your culture. It may not be your faith, but this is your place too.

"We are having a drive to be here for Londoners. We've been doing more late openings to get more locals, more Londoners, to see their cathedral." Also relatively new are the two pieces of video art by Bill Viola on the quire aisles. "Part of our role is to reinterpret the Christian message – the message is the same but the way you interpret it has to change as people's cultural understanding changes. Using the modern idiom of video is a way of making people stop and look in the way they wouldn't look at something static."

The dean summarises: "St Paul's is not an Establishment place; that's down in Westminster Abbey. St Paul's has always had a reputation for being edgy and taking risks." Indeed, anyone meeting David Ison is struck by his ability to move with the times, yet remain grounded in a deep belief in inclusivity, community and traditional Christian values.

St Paul's Cathedral at dusk

The choir stalls at St Paul's,
where evensong is conducted

MARCUS DAVEY

CEO AND ARTISTIC DIRECTOR,
THE ROUNDHOUSE

'You have to be able to have a dream that will turn everything upside down'

When Marcus Davey left his post at the Norfolk & Norwich Festival to join the Roundhouse, the festival chief paid tribute in a speech by saying: "Marcus has his head in the clouds and his feet on the ground." This certainly sums up his life in the period since he joined the Roundhouse, when it was simply a plot of land attached to an extraordinary idea. Almost two decades on, the vision has been turned into reality with plans for much more development to come. Marcus himself puts it this way: "You have to be able to have a dream that will turn everything upside down, but you also have to find a way to make it happen."

Nowadays the Roundhouse is flourishing, but it has not always been so. Built in the 19th century, it was a steam-engine maintenance shed before serving for roughly 100 years as a bonded warehouse for wines and spirits. The building fell into disuse until the dramatist Arnold Wesker resuscitated it in 1966 as a centre for the arts. After initial success it started to struggle: "I think Britain's view of counterculture in the early 1980s was at odds with Margaret Thatcher's view of how the world should be working and there was a lack of funding, a lack of appetite, and it fizzled out, unfortunately."

The Roundhouse, located in Chalk Farm, northwest London, closed in 1983 and it wasn't until 1996, when the businessman Sir Torquil Norman bought it, that real hope for a lasting cultural hub emerged. Marcus is full of praise for Sir Torquil: "He put in a huge amount of effort and got it done. It wasn't a glorification project for him, it was a glorification project to enable young people to get a better future.

"We need more people like him to put in not only the time and the effort but also money and contacts. I'm sure most of his friends walked on the other side of the street when they saw him coming because they knew he'd be asking for money. A lot of them were really generous, actually."

Marcus joined in 1999 and although in some ways the run-up to the Roundhouse reopening in 2006 was a marathon journey, there's no doubt it ended in an adrenalin-fuelled sprint. "The last week was sheer determination, mixed with terror and madness. On June 1, 2006, we were due to open. At the start of the day, we didn't have any of the licences or sign-offs, we didn't have the completion certificate from the architect, we didn't have anything.

"The Roundhouse was filled with builders and cleaners. The front door was due to be opened at 5pm. I was getting a bit stressed and I had people coming up to me with this and that. I was like a queen bee. Then the operations director came up to me and said, 'Here's a key.' I said, 'Yes, I can see that,' and he said, 'Can you just come and check it out please.' I was getting a bit wound up and I'm not that kind of person normally, but I had been having 20-hour days for the past six months.

"The operations director persisted, 'Can you just open the door?' I unlocked the door and pushed it open. And he said, 'There you go, you've just reopened the Roundhouse.' I burst into tears, and at that moment the whole team appeared with champagne. The whole thing had been a set-up."

At 7.30pm, the first show began. It was Fuerza Bruta, an Argentine company that ran for 13 weeks and sold out completely. The Roundhouse's emphasis on youth was there

from the start – the supporting show was The Foolish Young Man, which featured a cast of youngsters performing with David Harewood.

Many people hear the name the Roundhouse and think of it as only a music and entertainment venue. In fact, it is the largest creative centre for young people in the UK. In the past year alone, 5,000 have made use of its state-of-the-art studios, workshops, courses and programmes.

Over the years, 11 to 25 year olds have benefited from its resources not just in the music sphere but also in digital, broadcasting and the performing arts. "If you go to the BBC, I could probably introduce you to 30 or 40 of the staff of Radio 1 and Radio 1Xtra who came through the Roundhouse," says Marcus. "I could introduce you to team members in nearly every production company, I could probably name half the spoken-word artists out there and my colleagues would probably be able to name the other half. They've all been associated with the Roundhouse. The impact has been phenomenal."

Marcus has two roles: artistic director and chief executive. He jokes: "We often have arguments. 'You can't have the money.' 'Yes, I can!'" But as you speak to him, it becomes clear the roles are symbiotic. You are immediately struck by how he blends calmness with energy, passion with clear-headedness. Marcus is open to new ideas yet has a strong view about the way forward. Business skills are in harmony with creative vision.

When not working, he enjoys many of the free pursuits that London has to offer, such as visiting Kenwood House, walking up Primrose Hill, and taking in the views from the bridges across the Thames. The Roundhouse is never far from his thoughts, though: "It still trips me up to think that I was part of the team that reopened the Roundhouse. I still get caught in the throat when I talk about that day.

"To be here all those years, and to see a moment when a young person comes in – frightened and shy or worried and confused – to see them flourish, I could tell you a thousand stories of that and every one of them would get you in your heart."

In rehearsal, Club Swizzle
at the Roundhouse

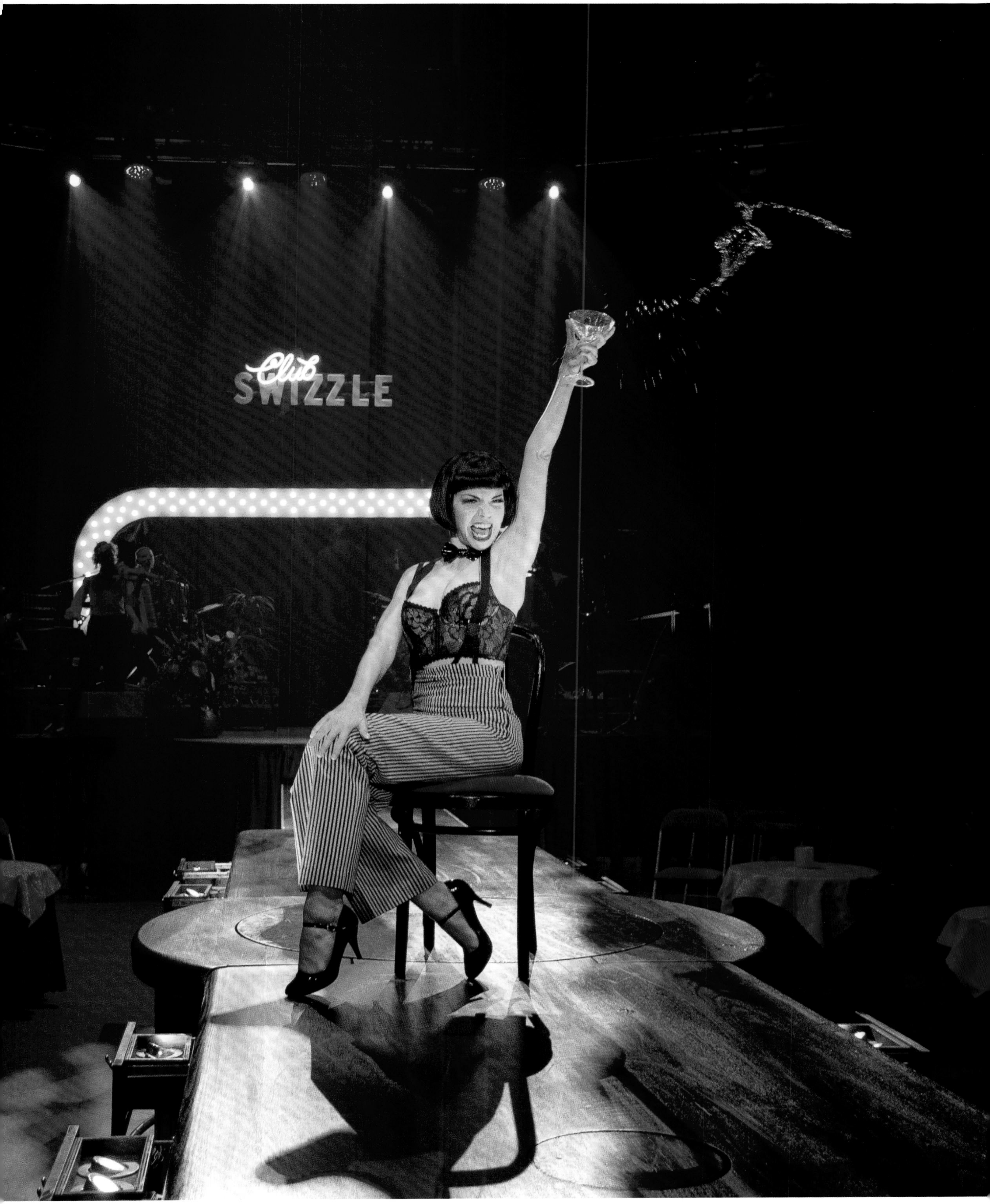
Club
SWIZZLE

FRANCIS OUTRED

CHAIRMAN AND HEAD OF
POST-WAR & CONTEMPORARY ART, CHRISTIE'S

'It's really exciting how different cultures come to play in the capital'

Francis Outred is a man steeped in the spirit of London. No matter which part of the capital it is, north, south, east or west, he's lived there at some point and he still enthuses about the city. In the 1970s and '80s, his father had a shop which was part of the Furniture Cave on the King's Road in Chelsea, specialising in 18th and 19th-century pieces. Francis helped out at weekends and recalls that all sorts of people came to visit, including future Formula 1 boss Bernie Ecclestone and the actor Roger Moore, who once politely asked to use the lavatory in his best James Bond voice.

Francis's mother was a senior producer at BBC World Service, and he credits both parents with developing his interest in current affairs and the art world. However, it was Mr Crook, his pottery teacher at King's College School in Wimbledon, who kindled the passion and pointed in the direction that led to him studying at Chelsea School of Art.

"A lot of what I do now involves trying to find new ways to do things, and art school stood me in good stead because you were told to just get on with it and left to your own devices, with unstructured but very invigorating lectures on a whole variety of topics. It was about working out what your own position in the world was," says Francis.

When he left in 1995, it was an exciting time for the British art world, largely fuelled by the opening of the Saatchi Gallery 10 years earlier. In his last year at Chelsea, inspired by the school's self-starter philosophy, Francis organised an exhibition including his own work in Hamburg. He organised further exhibitions in London, Paris, Berlin and Lisbon and so it evolved that his own art took more of a back seat, and

he became more of a show organiser and curator. In 1999 this path led him to take a job at Sotheby's. Francis explains: "I'd gone to auction houses as a student, even though it was not the done thing, but I had always been fascinated by different strands of the art world. For most artists and art students, the auction houses were perceived as somehow the dark side of the art world, but I didn't mind dancing there. It was free, you could just walk in and you never knew what you would find on the wall."

It was rare for someone with an artist's background to join one of the London auction houses but Francis arrived at time of change, bringing more of a systematic, curatorial approach. He set about establishing greater dialogues with the artists themselves, checking that they were happy with the way their works were presented both in catalogues and exhibitions.

He also initiated the concept of the private sale department, which could offer a more bespoke selection of sale options to private clients. The business was elaborating and becoming more complex as it expanded globally and beyond its traditional base of dealers as clients to a more panoramic view of the art world, with London at its centre. The breaking down of boundaries between galleries, museums, artists, collectors and auction houses enabled the creative business environment in which Francis thrives.

It was also around this time, roughly 10 years before Francis made the switch from Sotheby's, that the quintessentially English Christie's, founded in 1766, was bought by the French billionaire François Pinault's holding company.

Nowadays, New York is probably the dominant commercial

art city, closely followed by London, though the business is becoming increasingly international, particularly with the rise of Asia. "It is much more a global conversation," Francis says. "It used to be movements in regions, such as British art in the 1990s, but I'm not sure we'll see a city-based movement again. We'll see much more of a global groundswell of interests, with artists in different cities communicating and interacting with others around the world. London is a representation of that because we have great cultural diversity with wonderful galleries, museums and art schools."

He is fully aware of the increasing importance of the internet. "Christie's biggest challenge in the next 10 years is to make the experience of looking at art online almost like it is real." However, he counsels: "Geography will always be important. Buying art is part of a general leisure experience. You want to go to London to eat in nice restaurants, stay in nice hotels, see your friends and go to the auction house to buy something. The impact on London as an art centre could be just as badly felt by a drop in the quality of its general cultural and tourist offerings, its ambience and atmosphere, as by any development in the art world."

The auction market is thriving. "I said 10 years ago I would see a $1 billion work in my lifetime and I had a lot of stick, but it's already beginning to come true. When I made the statement, the record for a work of art was $85 million. Last year we sold a Leonardo da Vinci for $450 million. The first £1 million artwork – a Velázquez – was sold in 1970, now they are two a penny. Back then there were very few millionaires in the world, now there are about 250 billionaires."

Talking to Francis, one is struck by his insights into not just the art world but life generally. He admits he is concerned about the quality of what is being created: "It is more and more difficult for artists to seal themselves off from the machinations and temptations of the art market. The temptation to supply a specific demand has to have an impact on the product. The contemporary art scene is very different to how it was 20 years ago." He nevertheless is thoroughly positive about the way London is developing: "The great thing is that it is always changing. I'm excited by the transformation of places like St Pancras and Borough Market. There are areas that were very rundown when I was a teenager and are now very attractive. It's really exciting how different cultures come to play in the capital."

Similarly, the drama of a night-time auction captivates Francis as much as ever: "Our business is built towards creating a perfect moment for 60 works of art in an evening. No matter how much you do, no matter how you prepare, anything could happen in that minute of an auction. It's real-life theatre."

The drama of a Christie's sale as an Andy Warhol artwork reaches nearly £20m

STEVEN McRAE

PRINCIPAL DANCER, THE ROYAL BALLET

'The vibe in London is that ambition is celebrated, and I love that'

Anybody who knows Steven McRae cannot help but be inspired by his rare combination of dedication and hard work on the one hand and a balanced, thoughtful approach to life on the other. He was born in Sydney, Australia, and grew up in a motorsports family. His parents honeymooned at a racetrack and his father raced drag cars at 300mph. At first glance, it may seem a long way from the world of ballet, but Steven remembers being struck by his father's passion and love for the sport. This would be something that resonated with him throughout his life.

His sister was a gymnast, who also danced, and at just seven years old Steven told his parents that he too wanted to dance. He was lucky that not only did they support him in his desire but also that his early dance tutors gave him an absolute sense of freedom: "My teachers were incredible. Right from day one they said jump as high as you can, turn as fast as you can, be free. Doesn't matter if you're not perfect, we'll fix it later, just be free."

His parents did, though, insist that his academic studies come first. This meant long, intense days as Steven would dance on top of his normal school routine and at weekends too. He describes himself as incredibly competitive and says this was typical in his home country. "Everything was a competition. Australia was the top at every sport."

He welcomes what he sees as a complete shift in London's attitude. "At the time I arrived I felt ambition was frowned upon, it was almost vulgar. Since the Olympics in 2012, however, the vibe in London and in Britain is that ambition is celebrated, and I love that. I think the Olympics and the

success of the British team allowed people to openly say this is what I really want to achieve and that is what I'm aiming for."

After taking the Australian equivalent of GCSEs, Steven decided to pursue ballet full-time, much to the disappointment of his school, which assured him that he would regret it. He danced in the opening ceremony of the Sydney Olympics in 2000 and, aged just 15, spent a week in New York with the show Tap Dogs, but decided to choose ballet rather than go down the musical theatre route.

In 2003, Steven's life would change dramatically when he won the prestigious Prix de Lausanne and with it a scholarship to the ballet school of his choice. He had no hesitation in picking the Royal Ballet School in London, and its then director, Gailene Stock, happened to be in the Swiss city as head of the competition jury. She said to him: "Come tomorrow, don't go back to Australia." Thus, just turned 17 and having never lived away from home, he caught a plane to London.

He had terrible homesickness, but stuck it out and after 18 months joined the Royal Ballet company, where he had an early chance to shine. When he was 20, there were several injuries in the company and he was asked to perform the male lead in Romeo and Juliet with just five days to learn the part. He pulled it off. Steven says of that performance: "I will hold on to it for ever. It was an out-of-body experience."

Now over his homesickness, his mental strength was tested again when he suffered a partial rupture of his Achilles tendon, which kept him off stage for a year. Some surgeons said he would never dance again, but Steven being Steven wasn't

going to accept that. He progressed to first artist in 2005, to soloist in 2006, first soloist in 2008 and then a principal in 2009.

When he first arrived in the city, London was a culture shock. Now, he says: "I've morphed into a hybrid of Aussie and British." His wife, Elizabeth Harrod, a soloist of the Royal Ballet, is British and they have two young children, Audrey and Frederick. "Fatherhood is by far my best achievement," Steven says, but it has not dented his dancing ambitions, far from it. "I have more responsibility to lead by example."

Being a parent has also made him better at time management, and helped him to enjoy life more. He certainly has a full schedule. On a typical day, after the morning routine with the children, he arrives at the Royal Opera House in Covent Garden at about 9.30am and starts an intense warm-up. An hour later there is ballet class, which he likens to giving your car a grease and oil change. It's a time for improving technique, ironing out niggles, and getting your body back in alignment. Then, from midday to 5.30pm or 6.30pm, depending on whether there is a performance that night, he rehearses for three to eight productions. And then many evenings there will be a performance as well, taking it beyond a 12-hour working day. As he notes, it's an "insanely tough schedule".

Not only does the Australian love London and ballet dancing, he loves the Royal Ballet. He believes it's a real feather in Britain's cap that the company consistently attracts talent from all over the world. "Every time I step on that stage I am holding the hand of someone who is truly world class. That is something I still get excited by every single day. When you work in an institution like this you are surrounded by the world's leading artists. That is something Londoners should celebrate. The Royal Ballet is a bubbling pot of creativity.

"I'm very fortunate," he adds. "The Royal Ballet and the Royal Opera House have been a huge part of my life, they believed in me." Fortunate, perhaps, but as Steven himself notes: "Success is a three-legged stool: hard work, talent and luck."

The Young Dancer by Enzo Plazzotta
sits opposite the Royal Opera House

GERARD MENAN

MANAGER, GORDON'S WINE BAR

'I'm a Londoner first, Frenchman second'

At first glance Gerard Menan strikes one as the quintessential Frenchman, but on further inspection it is not so simple. "I'm a Londoner first, Frenchman second," states this charming Anglophile, who was born and brought up in Segré in the Loire Valley.

Gerard worked in the catering business in France before crossing the channel in 1989 to improve his English. The plan was to stay for a year or two; 29 years later he is still here. After three months working in a kitchen in St Albans, Hertfordshire, he arrived in London on January 1, 1990. He was manager of The Village in Hammersmith, frequented by the Countess of Wessex (then Sophie Rhys-Jones), and later worked at the Sheraton Park Tower hotel.

Gerard believes the timing of his arrival in London was very fortunate. He recalls it as a vibrant time for the capital, with many restaurants and bars changing to a more continental style. It was also, fortuitously, when more and more Londoners were developing a taste for wine.

He visited Gordon's, London's oldest wine bar, in 1991 and fell in love with it. Nearly 10 years later he was delighted when he was offered the opportunity to work there, as assistant manager. Since becoming manager Gerard has changed very little about the atmospheric wine bar and kept alive its tradition of providing quality wines and cheeses.

One big change, though, was putting seats and tables on the terrace outside. The bright open-air area adjoins Victoria Embankment Gardens and provides a counterpoint to the intimate interior of the subterranean bar.

There has also been a change in the clientele, says Gerard.

"It used to be like a gentlemen's club, now it is much younger, many more ladies. You have all kinds of society coming to Gordon's and they all respect each other. It has always attracted people who prefer to be somewhere with character rather than going to a big chain." The business has grown throughout his tenure. One factor has been the number of tourists since the London 2012 Olympics, when he was interviewed by media from around the world.

The bar has been a feature of London life since its establishment in 1890 by Angus Gordon. Rudyard Kipling lived upstairs in the same building and wrote his novel The Light That Failed while there. GK Chesterton also wrote some of his works in the bar. Further back in time, before Gordon's opened its doors, Samuel Pepys lived in the building in the 1680s.

It is still a favourite haunt of London's theatre community, partly attracted by the intimate and quirky environment (pictured overleaf). Gordon's is strictly first come, first served and only takes bookings for the Cage, an area for 8-10 people in the old wine cellar.

Gerard's mornings are spent on day-to-day business matters, sorting the bureaucracy. As he says: "There is lots to think about. Glasses, for example; if we don't have enough glasses, we don't drink a bottle of wine with a straw!"

He is full of funny phrases and has a ready smile on his face, always seeing the bright side of life. When he first came to London the weather was a challenge. "Oh my God, I thought the sun had disappeared." But now even the weather is much better, he says.

PHILIP GRIFFITHS

ACTOR, THE PHANTOM OF THE OPERA

*'I've done over 11,000 performances –
eight shows a week, 416 shows a year'*

Philip Griffiths is a record-breaker. In 2016 he was officially recognised by Guinness World Records as the longest-serving cast member of a West End production. He started in The Phantom of the Opera at Her Majesty's Theatre in 1990 and continues to extend his record, playing two parts – the auctioneer and Monsieur Reyer.

Philip calculates: "Eight shows a week, 416 shows a year. Allowing for holidays, I have done over 11,000 performances. When I'm waiting to go on I do still get a buzz. After all, in each performance there are 1,200 people seeing me for the first time."

At first blush this amazing achievement may seem a far cry from Philip's upbringing in a farming family in the village of Caersws in Montgomeryshire. "We didn't have a television until I was a teenager, and then it didn't work very well because there was a hill at the back of the house and there was terrible reception. We ended up taking the aerial on to the top of the hill and it was fantastic."

However, Philip was always drawn towards singing. "We're born singing in Wales and my parents had lovely voices but knew nothing about show business They didn't have a clue what I was going in for, but the family were supportive." Philip competed regularly in Eisteddfods and then, at 17, he auditioned successfully for Royal Manchester College of Music. Borrowing his uncle's car, his parents took him to Manchester. It was Philip's first time outside Wales: "We went down a dual carriageway and I really thought we were on a motorway. I'd never seen two lanes before!"

During his four years in Manchester he met his wife,

the opera singer Susanna Ross. They both then joined the Glyndebourne Festival Opera company. A highlight from that period came when the company was invited to perform Don Giovanni directed by Peter Hall at the National Theatre in London. "Right across from our dressing room was Sir John Gielgud's room and I can remember his butler, with his white gloves, polishing the glasses ready for the guests that were coming. I left the dressing room to go on stage and who was coming towards me but Sir John, and he looked at me and said, 'Good luck, my boy,' in that beautiful plummy voice."

In 1978, Philip made the switch to musical theatre. "I had shied away from it. I really wish I'd tried it earlier." His early forays into musicals gave no hint of the longevity to come. Kings and Clowns lasted a month at the Phoenix Theatre in London's West End and The Biograph Girl did only a little better, managing six weeks at the same theatre. Philip shrugged off the disappointment, "I was so thrilled to be working in London. Everybody wants to come to London, and even more so now than in 1978. I think London is the international capital of the world. And, of course, there is nowhere to touch our theatre. The level of the people we have performing here and the theatres we've got are fantastic."

He then appeared in a string of hits at the Prince Edward Theatre: Evita, Chess and Anything Goes. In 1990, he successfully auditioned for The Phantom of the Opera and thought: "Crikey, I've got to see it now!" The show had opened in 1986 and Philip's first day coincided with its fourth anniversary. "In those days there were six-monthly contracts and you never knew how long you were going to be around.

I'm still here after 28 years and I'm still thinking this could be the last one," he jokes.

Playing the parts of the auctioneer and Monsieur Reyer involves logistics of military precision. "As soon as I finish as the auctioneer, I leave the podium, go round through a pass door and there's a team of people waiting there: somebody from wardrobe, somebody from sound and somebody from wigs with a tin containing my sideburns and moustache, which are taped on because we haven't got time for glue. My microphone has to go in my hat, and I have to get all that done in time to sing the chorus of Hannibal. It's a very quick change."

Philip credits three main people with bringing the show to life: the costume and set designer Maria Bjornson ("that woman was just a genius"), the director Hal Prince and the choreographer Dame Gillian Lynne. As well as his regular roles, Philip is an understudy for Monsieur André, whom he loves playing when he gets the chance. Philip has many highlights from his run in the show. He recalls the time when Princess Diana came with her sons. Unaware in advance, the cast soon heard whispers. "Well, of course, the minute we knew where she was sitting we all had to have a little peek. Apparently, it was one of her favourite shows."

Another favourite memory is from 1991 when there was a celebration to mark the fact that Andrew Lloyd Webber had six shows on in the West End at the same time: Cats, Aspects of Love, Starlight Express, Joseph and the Amazing Technicolor Dreamcoat, Jesus Christ Superstar and, of course, The Phantom of the Opera. "Six shows is unbelievable. We all got into our costumes and a bus collected us and took us to the Palladium. There was a big dais on stage and Andrew sat in the middle with all of us surrounding him. That was a very special event. That's not going to happen again."

Philip and his wife Susanna have two daughters who are now grown up, so he doesn't have the early starts he used to. Both children are very musical. The first, Anna, was born just after Philip went into Evita and she learnt to play the piano and read music by herself, working it out from the score. Her sister Siân is studying singing at Guildhall School of Music.

Philip lives in Lewes, near the Sussex coast. He tends to leave for home straight after the performance and, fittingly, "as I walk past the church clock on our road, it is striking midnight". Also appropriate is the fact that The Phantom of the Opera is at Her Majesty's Theatre, as previously there was an opera house on the site.

"The Phantom of the Opera is iconic," says Philip. "When it opened in 1986 it was a huge success and it has become part of London life, along with Les Misérables, Wicked and shows like that. They're the reason many people come here."

Light trails from a passing bus outside
Her Majesty's Theatre on Haymarket

10.35pm
A view from the South Bank across the
Thames towards Victoria Embankment

CHRISTINA DEY

ROAD SPACE INFORMATION OFFICER,
LONDON STREETS TRAFFIC CONTROL CENTRE

'Our department is here to keep the city moving'

When you exit the security pod and enter the large open-plan office that is the London Streets Traffic Control Centre, you feel like you are in a futuristic nerve centre from a Hollywood blockbuster. Straight ahead is the Core, a space dominated by a bank of screens showing live CCTV images of traffic, maps of the city full of coloured lines and symbols, and a 24-hour news channel.

As a road space information officer, Christina Dey has a number of roles, one of which is to work on the Core. "If you get a call for an incident you can use the cameras to identify and locate what's happening and its level of impact. There are 5,000 CCTV cameras all over London, which we can access and a lot of them we can move round 360 degrees. We're just looking at traffic issues; we don't get involved in things such as criminal offences."

The Core desk can get particularly busy. Calls come from the police, highways officials and contractors, giving information about problems on the roads. The city is divided into north, south, east and centre. If there's a collision on the A406 it goes to the team covering the north, a collision in Clapham goes to south.

"Obviously it's real time and you have to speedily update the website, create incidents and update Twitter," says Christina. "When multiple incidents happen at the same time you still have to be productive, you still have to communicate across all of the channels. I've had several incidents on the Core where the phones are ringing, you've more calls coming in and contractors, who maintain the roads, are ringing up for each of those incidents wanting updates. One day was so busy that I got nominated for an award for my excellent performance."

Christina was born and raised in south London and has spent her professional life in public service. She did a BTEC in media at the BRIT School for Performing Arts and Technology and then a BSc in communications technology at Ravensbourne College. She worked on asylum-seekers' cases at the Home Office, followed by 10 years with the police answering emergency calls.

"You get all manner of calls on 999. I remember on my training, they put us in a room and gave us some sample calls. It's quite nerve-wracking, worrying that you are going to be on the other end of the phone to somebody who may be in a life or death situation, then they called up from the next room saying, 'Hello, my cat's stuck up a tree,'" laughs Christina.

While waiting for security clearance from the police for that job, she spent two years as an air hostess and did youth work for the Prince's Trust.

Christina started at the London Streets Traffic Control Centre three years ago. Even in that short time, Twitter has become extremely important. She uses it to respond to enquiries about incidents and to give out information. The account @tfltrafficnews has grown quickly to more than 1.4 million followers. There's a lot of noise on Twitter, though. "You have to weed out the good bits where you can be constructive. There are people who want to be negative or goad you into a conversation but you don't engage with them," Christina says.

She and the rest of the traffic control centre team limit the disruption to road users by being effective with the flow

The traffic co-ordinators can change the length of time any of London's 6,300 traffic lights are green or red

of information, but there are other tools that they use as well. For example, the traffic co-ordinators can remotely change the length of time that any of London's 6,300 sets of traffic lights are green or red. The centre can also ensure that the police get out to direct traffic at important locations. "Our department is here to keep London moving. My job is varied, rewarding, challenging and unique," says Christina.

It's a 24-hour operation. The shifts are: 6.30am to 2pm; 2pm to 9.30pm; and 9.30pm to 6.30am. Once every four months, Christina does seven nights in a row. Normally she goes straight home to bed, but it has been known for her to leave work at 6.30am to have her hair done, which takes about six hours, and not get to bed until the afternoon.

On days when she has free time, she enjoys walking around London and taking in the sights. "I've been on the London Eye loads of times. I enjoy the South Bank. I love the Science Museum and the Museum of Childhood in Bethnal Green. I also like going to the parks, such as Richmond. I love London. I can't imagine being anywhere else unless it's somewhere very sunny, but even then I'd need to have a base here."

Information from 5,000 CCTV cameras
helps to keep traffic flowing

11.15pm
London Bridge is the fourth
busiest station in Britain

GIULIANO MORANDIN

BAR MANAGER, THE DORCHESTER

'I've always loved the bar, it was my calling'

If you happen to be in Park Lane in the early hours of the morning and see a tall, elegant gentleman with a dapper moustache get on a Vespa and start heading south from The Dorchester, more likely than not it will be the hotel's award-winning bar manager, Giuliano Morandin, making his way home from work.

Giuliano was born in a small town close to Padua in Italy in 1953. His father was a plumber, but Giuliano opted to attend catering college, where he was taught English, French and German as well as learning the technical side of the industry.

Since the age of 14 he had worked front of house in restaurants and bars. "I've always loved the bar, it was my calling. I like the buzz, the feeling, the action, and people always seem to be happier at the bar."

After graduating, he went to Bonn and soon found himself behind a bar again. When Giuliano asked the bar manager why he had selected him for the job, he was told: "You're the only one who carries the tray on the left. Everybody else carries it on the right and then they go to open the door and they can't open it."

In Bonn, he served the likes of Indira Gandhi and Emperor Hirohito. He then had a spell in a German seaside resort on the Baltic, but he wanted to move to England. "London was always a magnet for me. London was a happening place."

Giuliano and some friends arrived in the capital and first found work in the Hilton, then decided to see some of the world, joining the Swedish American Line. He gravitated back to London, mainly because he had met his wife-to-be there and was missing her.

They duly married. Giuliano smiles as he thinks of his wife's father: "He's funny, the way he talks about the war, 'I was torpedoed twice, sunk …I had a wonderful war.' He must like swimming!" Giuliano went back to the Hilton, then worked at Duke's hotel for about six years before being appointed head barman at The Dorchester, where he has been ever since, apart from a short stint at The Berkeley when The Dorchester was having a refurbishment.

For Giuliano, being a legendary bar manager is about more than mixing delicious cocktails. "You have to make people feel welcome. People trust you and empty their souls to you. You are a friend, a confessor, but you always have to be professional. The way I look at it, if someone comes in here they are like a guest in my home – unfortunately, I have to give them the bill."

That's not to say he does not take particular care with his cocktails as well. "When we reopened The Bar at The Dorchester 12 years ago, we wanted a signature drink. We wanted to have something of historical value and we chose the Martinez. It was originally made with Old Tom gin, but there was none on the market, so we recreated it." The botanicals in the gin, which is exclusive to The Dorchester, include juniper, coriander, angelica root, orris root, cassia bark, cardamom, fresh lemon and orange peel.

Giuliano is not only charismatic but self-effacing. He is effusive about the team, saying: "We have achieved what we have achieved together." Many of the staff have been there for over a decade. Most notable is Simon Rowe, who, like Giuliano, has been at The Dorchester for over 30 years.

The Dorchester's customers have included people such as Nelson Mandela, Woody Allen and Barbra Streisand

Altogether, the bar team have clocked up more than 100 years at the hotel.

Giuliano's day starts at 5pm, when he deals with all the paperwork. The bar closes at 1am (midnight on Sundays), and he leaves at 2.30am. He loves his work at The Dorchester, and loves his adopted city: "London for me is the best place in the world. We all get on with each other, people blend in, there is a respect, a sense of what is fair, and the city is evolving. I feel Italian but I feel like I'm an Italian from London. I've always felt welcome."

He, in turn, believes in making everyone feel welcome at The Dorchester. "Deep down everybody wants to be treated for the person they are, not their title, not their money."

While The Dorchester's customers have included the world's royalty as well as notable people such as Nelson Mandela, Woody Allen, Barbra Streisand, Diana Ross and Arnold Schwarzenegger, Giuliano Morandin believes in treating everybody the same. "Everybody pays the same money and they share the same space. It doesn't matter who the customer is, our job is to please."

The Bar at The Dorchester on Park Lane

PAUL MURPHY

JOINT OWNER, YES CHEF

'I've been all over the world, but nothing compares to London'

Paul Murphy brims with energy and bonhomie, which is all the more striking given that we meet at 9am and he has been up working since midnight at New Covent Garden market. Although he moved to Essex as a boy, he is a Londoner through and through. He was born in Newham, his father came from Islington and his mother from Bethnal Green.

Paul is a fourth-generation greengrocer. He recalls his grandfather, Fred, telling stories of going to the original Covent Garden fruit and vegetable market with his father, Paul's great-grandfather, on a horse and cart with their buying list scrawled on the back of a paper bag.

Danny Murphy, Paul's father, started his career in the old market in the 1950s as a banana cutter. Paul explains: "The bananas used to come over on the plant in those days – they were called coffins – and Dad used to cut the bananas off. Then he became a porter, pulling the wooden barrows – the market was full of cobblestones. But then with the introduction of the HGV lorries, the cornering was too tight and the forklift trucks didn't work on the cobblestones, so they built New Covent Garden."

The replacement, on the south side of the Thames in Nine Elms, was a far cry from the old market, not just in terms of distance. "The first day Dad drove over the Thames, he claimed to have cried as the new market used to look a bit like a prison." That was 1974 and the surrounding area has since seen a massive change. "It's been redeveloped and it's like a mini Dubai or Canary Wharf," says Paul. In 2015, work started on redeveloping the market itself. "I've got great hopes for it," he says. "There's going to be a walkway through

the market, it's going to involve the public more and have multimillion-pound tower blocks above us."

Back in 1984, Danny Murphy set up Chef's Connection to supply fruit and vegetables to restaurants. Initially, Paul was not destined to join the family business. He was having a terrific time as a ski instructor in the Alps, the USA and Canada, and also earning money by dancing on stage at raves. "In 1990, my Dad said you've had enough messing about – it wasn't messing about to me, it was a job – and asked me to come into the business, which I did. It grew into one of the biggest fruit and vegetable distribution companies in London, employing over 100 people."

Chef's Connection started off just supplying the likes of Pierre Koffmann, Marco Pierre White, Gordon Ramsay, Gary Rhodes, Angela Hartnett and Giorgio Locatelli, but as it expanded it took on bigger and bigger customers. "Maybe we got a little too successful because everybody wanted us to supply them," says Paul. "If I'm being honest, we took our eye off the bespoke work, which we got too big to look after.

"We were doing every high street chain, including Café Rouge, whose first restaurant was actually started by my mum and dad. When they sold the restaurant, part of the deal was that we would supply all the Café Rouges the new owners opened up and we ended up supplying about 78 of them. Those owners sold out for an incredible sum of money to Whitbread – Dad always said he sold the business 77 restaurants too soon!"

Financial difficulties started to surface and Chef's Connection was restructured. In 2013, the Murphy family

left and the following year established Yes Chef with Martin Wheeler. The company focuses on the personal touch and does not supply large chains. Instead, it serves anything from Michelin-starred restaurants to gastropubs.

New Covent Garden as a whole supplies all the top 20 restaurants in London and 40% of all the city's fruit and vegetables eaten outside the home. Everything is geared to getting chefs' orders ready early each morning. Yes Chef opens at 7pm, taking orders by email and phone. "The guys come in and start packing, everything gets weighed up and then at 2am or 3am the drivers start coming in," Paul says. "The orders get checked on to the back of the trucks, and we try to get the trucks out by 5am because every chef wants his order by 7am. Then the trucks start coming back, they're washed and we do second deliveries. We close the office at 3pm."

The restaurant industry is hard work for everyone involved. "All of us live on very little sleep – whether you're in the fish game, the meat game or a chef or a waiter." Yes Chef operates six days a week and sometimes it comes to the rescue of customers who are open Sunday and need something desperately.

Paul is amazed by the regeneration of London. "There are all these areas where before you wouldn't want to walk and now you can't afford to buy there; places that our parents or grandparents moved out of to get away from, you couldn't afford to move back into. I've been all over the world. Yes, there are some other great cities, but for me nothing compares to London."

He sees parallels between the changes taking place generally in the capital and the improvements in the food scene. "All the different nationalities that are here now, it's fantastic. When I came into the business 28 years ago, it was your Sunday roast vegetables and your oranges and your plums and pineapples. Now it's thousands of different products you could be asked for. It's a really good time to be in London and in food in London."

Citrus fruit makes a colourful display
at New Covent Garden market

SAMMY MINZLY

PARTNER, BEIGEL BAKE

*'We learnt the proper way
and we are the original'*

Sammy Minzly is one of the partners who own the famous 24-hour Beigel Bake on Brick Lane in London's East End. Our chat was conducted in unusual circumstances: the bakery adjoins the shop and, with no chairs available, we squatted on our haunches amid the beigel-making machinery. Sammy started by asking if I was "secure". "Secure?" I asked. "Yes," he explained, as he pointed around me. "This is a machine, and this, and this too."

The room was filled not only with equipment, but with a fantastic smell of baking. There was a terrific bonhomie as the staff traded good-natured banter with Sammy while they worked around us.

It's no wonder Sammy is popular. He is a charming, friendly, slightly understated man in his early eighties. Born in Israel, he came to London in 1958 and initially worked in Willesden as a driver delivering bread for a bakery. In the mid-1970s, he and his partners saw an opportunity to sell beigels wholesale and soon after to the public. What started as a steady trickle of hungry black-cab drivers late at night slowly but surely built up into a stream of customers sufficient to keep the shop busy 24 hours a day.

Of course, while Beigel Bake – pictured overleaf – remains a staple feature of Brick Lane, the area around the shop has changed substantially. Initially populated largely by the Jewish community, the 1980s saw many of them leave the East End and move out to north London. Meanwhile, Bengali families, shopkeepers and restaurant owners arrived. Since the 1990s, the area has gentrified to a degree and become trendy.

Beigel Bake's customers these days come from all over the world. Tourists from Japan, China, New Zealand, Australia and the USA seek it out. Among the many notables coming from abroad have been Mariah Carey, Beyoncé and the actors behind the small-screen legends Fonzie (Henry Winkler) and Huggy Bear (Antonio Fargas).

Sammy is proud of the fact that the staff are multicultural too: "We employ all types: Arabs, Jews, Chinese, black, green, yellow." He is also proud of his beigels: "We learnt the proper way and we are the original. I'll tell you a secret: years ago, when people asked how do you make the hole in the beigel, we would say a man with a wooden leg would stamp on it. The truth is we make them with a machine that joins the ends together like a Polo Mint."

The shifts at Beigel Bake are long. Sammy, for example, comes in on Wednesday afternoon and leaves in the early hours of Thursday. "People ask why I don't retire but the truth is you need to get out of the house to stay healthy." Everything for sale in the shop is made by Beigel Bake itself – the bread, the rolls, the cakes and the 3,000 or so beigels baked each day.

The shop employs its own unique process, not sacrificing taste for speed. The beigels are boiled, baked, cooled, sliced and filled and it is reckoned that Beigel Bake gets through nearly 20,000 brown paper bags in an average week.

Right now, the beigel is very much in fashion and at weekends, in particular, the shop is filled with hungry foodies. I can see why. Before we left, Sammy was kind enough to insist that we take some beigels home with us, hot off the press. They were delicious!

ANTONIO POLLEDRI

JOINT OWNER OF THE FAMILY-RUN BAR ITALIA

'Soho has changed but it's still the most vibrant place in London'

Anyone who visited Bar Italia more than 50 years ago and returned today could be forgiven for thinking that time had stopped. While the surrounding streets of Soho have changed radically, the café has remained almost exactly the same since it was founded in 1949 by Lou and Caterina Polledri. Still there is the terrazzo floor, the red and white Formica bar counter, the same Gaggia coffee brewing machine, the same excellent Italian blend from Angelucci's and, perhaps most iconic of all, the Rocky Marciano boxing gloves and poster.

The heavyweight boxing champion liked to visit when in London and was a huge fan of Caterina's polenta and risotto. After his death, his wife sent the poster in gratitude. It has hung on the wall ever since – apart from when it featured in the 1980s film Absolute Beginners. The director, Julian Temple, reproduced the Soho of the Swinging Sixties at Shepperton Studios but was adamant that he had to have the original poster presented by Marciano's widow to the Polledris.

Four generations of the family have been involved in Bar Italia, and the Little Italy restaurant next door. Lou and Caterina, who hailed from Emilia-Romagna in northern Italy, were followed by their son Nino and his wife Vera. Nino was responsible for the café getting its practically 24-hour status and ensuring that Bar Italia was the first café to gain a licence until 5am. Today the founders' grandchildren – Antonio, brother Luigi and sister Veronica – run the show, with the help of their children.

When Lou and Caterina founded Bar Italia it was a social centre for the large Italian community then living in Soho. The café's continuing association with their home country is highlighted by the three World Cup finals featuring Italy that London-born Antonio – also known as Antony – has witnessed as an adult. Each time, there has been a party atmosphere outside with about 7,000 people thronging Frith Street. In 1982, when Italy played West Germany, disaster nearly struck, Antonio recalls. "The place was heaving and unfortunately, due to the heat of all the sweating Italians, the TV packed up and they all came for me – they wanted to lynch me. Fortunately we were able to run next door and borrow a TV, plug it in and keep them happy."

While Italians have been a permanent theme running through Bar Italia in particular, and Soho generally, there have been many transitions in the surrounding community. In the early days, Soho was a particularly edgy place, but in the 1980s the music industry reinvigorated it (Antonio likens it to the area moving from black and white to colour). Artists such as Sade and Adam Ant featured Bar Italia in their videos. Also, many sex shops in the area closed down and became coffee shops.

One of Antonio's favourite stories is how at 7am one day he got talking at Bar Italia to the film director Francis Ford Coppola, who became a regular customer. "He had this funny quirk where he always wanted to pay for everything in dollars. Each time the conversation seemed to finish with me saying, 'Don't worry, Mr Coppola, it's fine.' On the last day of his stay he wanted to take two cappuccino cups and saucers back to his mother in California. I gave them to him. He then pulled out some dollars and said, 'How much?' I said, 'Don't worry, it's an honour.' He said, 'I'm going back to my vineyard.

ROCKY MARC
Undefeated heavyweight champion

OPPONENT	DECISION	ROU'ND
LEE EPPERSON	KO	3
ARRY BALZERIAN	KO	1
OWARD	KO	1
IN	KO	3
SS	KO	1
EKS	KO	1
SON	KO	1
AN	KO	1
SON	KO	1
ELLY	KO	1
N	KO	2
ZIE	KO	5
	KO	
	KO	

When I return to London I'll bring you a bottle of wine.' Three weeks later, at seven in the morning, who comes bowling down the road? It's Mr Coppola. Opens his bag, pulls out a bottle of wine, written on the label – To my friend Antony, please enjoy this with your family, FFC."

Soho has become big business, with few independent and family outlets left. Antonio cites Algerian Coffee Stores, Lina Stores, Maison Bertaux and the French Pub among the few that remain, and he worries that with Crossrail coming soon, business rates will rise and the places that still give the area its village feel will also disappear. He is confident, though, that Bar Italia is well placed financially to maintain its place at the heart of Soho.

He has another story, however, about having to adapt to modern commercial requirements. American Express was launching a new charge card and used Bar Italia as the location for the advertising. "We got a lot of fantastic publicity. We were over the moon. Ten days after the launch, however, the ad agency phoned and said, 'We've got a problem. The CEO of American Express came down to Bar Italia with his friends and tried to pay and you refused his card.' I said, 'We don't take cards.' He said, 'Well, if you don't accept his card the next time he comes in, we're pulling the ad.'

"So, from then on every time someone wanted to pay with a card we ran next door to the restaurant, picked up its card machine and ran back to the customer. Eventually we had to succumb and get our own card machine."

The story of Bar Italia and its owners is an illustration of the wonderful resilience of passion. While all around them the world has changed at an ever-increasing pace, the family have upheld the values dating back to the launch in 1949 that have made the coffee bar such a popular place with Londoners and visitors alike.

Antonio reflects: "I'm very lucky that I've spent the best part of my life coming down to the place I love to be in. That's Soho, that's Bar Italia. I feel deeply privileged. It's a great place to sit and watch the world go by – day and night. You'll see the latest fashions, the best fashions. You'll also see the world's worst fashions. Soho has changed but it's still the most vibrant place in London."

Night owls at Bar Italia in Soho

3.45am
Piccadilly Circus at dawn after a typical London downpour

STEVE ALLEN

RADIO PRESENTER, LBC

'It's my life through a microphone'

"Dr Johnson was right," says Steve Allen, "When a man is tired of London he is tired of life." It would be hard to find a man more keen on London or his job than Steve. He was born in southeast England but had a peripatetic childhood because his father was in the armed forces, with two-year spells in Hong Kong, Egypt and Germany, as well Essex and Yorkshire in the UK. It is in stark contrast to his adult life, which has seen him remain as a presenter at LBC since 1979.

LBC was the first commercial radio station. Its first broadcast was at 6am on October 8, 1973. Steve Allen and Clive Bull are the only broadcasters from the old days in the current line-up. "All the rest of them have died or they're very old and retired," he chuckles. In its early days, LBC was based in Gough Square, home to Dr Johnson's House, nestled among a maze of courts and alleys just off Fleet Street.

It was very different from the state-of-the-art offices of the station's current owner, Global, in Leicester Square. In the 1970s there were no computers or mobile phones, and during phone-ins the producer would write the name of the caller on a piece of paper and hold it up to the glass for the presenter. Steve has not always had the early morning slot of 4am to 7am. At one time he worked the Night Extra show, from midnight until 5am, when there would be "what was laughingly called music to brighten your day – we called it music to slash your wrists to".

He learnt to fill hours of airtime by just talking, and never liked doing phone-in shows. "I'm rubbish at them. They tried to make me do them for a little while and the audience decided they didn't want to hear me doing phone-ins too!" These days, Steve arrives at LBC at 2.45am, records his daily podcast and scans the newspapers. But apart from the opening for each hour of the show, he never really knows what he is going to say.

"I like to test myself to see if I can go an hour and half without looking at a newspaper. I only fall back on the papers if I can't think of anything to talk about, which is rare." Indeed, regular listeners testify that Steve is a man who can natter away about his hanging baskets, a trip to Costco or his passion for prosecco for 10 minutes or more and still keep you interested. As he says: "It's my life through a microphone."

It's not, however, just his stories and anecdotes that listeners tune in for. Steve is known for his acerbic comments when it comes to Z-list celebrities, although he notes: "I think I've become more moderate over the years. I think I'm being quite nice to some of them. Sometimes I even go two days without mentioning Kerry Katona." He's not one for holidays. "I'm going to get up in the morning anyway, so I may as well work. I love my job; it's no hardship to sit down, have a chocolate biscuit and read the newspapers."

LBC went nationwide in 2014, and as Steve puts it: "The station can pull its weight and live with the big boys when it comes to covering big news events, but there is a nice lighter side to the station which is very human."

He still loves the city as much as ever. "I do all the touristy things like taking a river boat or visiting the Tower of London or St Paul's just to reaffirm that I'm in London." As for working at LBC: "I'm still as enthusiastic now as I ever was in the early days, it's just now I'm a bit better at it. Well, I think I am!"

A room at Dr Johnson's House in Gough Square in the City of London, the location where LBC was originally based

FREDA COKER-APPIAH

MIDWIFE, UNIVERSITY COLLEGE HOSPITAL

'In our training we had to do 40 deliveries. After that you just stop counting'

Freda Coker-Appiah is one of those rare people who light up a room with their smile. You immediately sense that you are in the presence of a warm, good-hearted person – valuable assets for a midwife, an occupation she was always drawn to.

Born in Ghana, Freda completed her degree and then came to Britain. After studying nursing in the Florence Nightingale School in King's College London, she worked at St Thomas' Hospital and then at St George's as a cardiac nurse. "When I was having a baby at the Royal Free Hospital, I had a very positive experience, and realised that I could follow my desire to be a midwife. I thought, I can do this. I saw some aspects of the job that suited me; for example, I like to talk!"

In 2004 she joined University College London Hospitals NHS Foundation Trust to train as a midwife. "You learn on the job, you're not sitting in a classroom," Freda says. "You go in the field and work hands on. In our training we had to do 40 deliveries. After that you just jump in and stop counting."

The Elizabeth Garrett Anderson Wing of University College Hospital moved to its current location 10 years ago. "In the old building, the labour ward had nine rooms, and it had two bathrooms, so when you delivered the baby and you wanted to go to the bathroom there was a scramble for who would get there first," Freda recalls.

The current building is a great advance, with 12 rooms, all en-suite, in the labour ward plus four rooms for close observation of women who are unwell or recovering from a Caesarean section. There's also another room for those not in labour but in need of monitoring. "It's a shiny building and a

lovely environment. It's sunnier and brighter than many other hospitals," she says.

As a midwife, Freda sees women through their pregnancies, advising them on matters such as diet, travel and exercise, then supports them when they are in labour. "You have to be everything – you are an advocate for the woman and also a friend, you make sure her delivery is safe, and you're also looking after the rest of the family. Afterwards you provide support when they are back at home, advising them on matters such as breast feeding and how to care for the baby. We follow them up for 10 to 15 days, then we hand over to the health visitor."

Freda works 12-hour shifts, starting at 8am or 8pm. The long shift is designed to provide continuity to the woman giving birth. "Our job is such that you can't just take off – sometimes you've been with the woman the whole day and then she's delivering just as you were going to go home. Midwives can't just take their bags and go. We end up staying to do the delivery and then the documentation. Although you are tired, at that point you are so happy."

A big difference from when Freda started as a midwife back in 2004 is the number of husbands and partners present at the birth. "It's frightening for a lot of men," she says. "For a lot of them their idea of giving birth comes from watching the telly, where it's five minutes, the mother screams, the baby's out and everybody's happy. So they can find overwhelming the reality of the long wait and the pain involved. I have to reassure and support them."

Freda has lived in London for about 20 years and considers

On average around 6,600 women give birth at UCH each year

it her home now. Before she came her impressions were based on books she had read. "I had read about winter, but I had never known it in Ghana," she says.

"If you are in a hot country and you read about autumn leaves, you can't imagine them, but once you are in London you really appreciate what the authors meant. I studied English literature and it brings me joy to walk around the likes of Waterloo and Westminster, and all the areas that I read about back in Ghana."

It's not just the weather and the places that are different, she adds. "In London, you meet people you would never meet anywhere else. We are such a diverse community. For example, coming from West Africa, I wouldn't have seen people from South Africa back there, but I meet them here. You meet everybody and it's lovely."

This is confirmed by the startling fact that the staff of UCLH are drawn from over 100 different nations. On average around 6,600 women give birth at the hospital each year, assisted by Freda and her colleagues. Those new arrivals come from a variety of backgrounds, but they are all *London Lives*.

The Elizabeth Garrett Anderson Memorial at the entrance to the maternity wing of UCLH. The artwork, by Carl Jaycock, is made up of images of staff past and present

Commuters stream
across London Bridge

AFTERWORD

ABOUT PERFECT PAIR PUBLISHING

London Lives is the first book from Perfect Pair Publishing and is produced by the company's founders, Danny Rosenbaum and Rupert Vandervell.

For many years, Danny made current affairs documentaries such as Dispatches and Trial & Error as well as being a producer for Channel 4 News, before setting up a web publishing company. Rupert worked at Condé Nast Publications for over two decades, where he became head of video production. He is an award-winning photographer.

If you enjoyed *London Lives* and want to hear about our future titles, you can email danny@perfectpairpublishing.com asking to be placed on our email list, or refer to our website 24londonlives.com. You can also follow us on Twitter or Instagram via @24londonlives.

Danny Rosenbaum and Rupert Vandervell

BLEY STADIUM, BA
ESTY'S THEATRE, BA
HOUSE, EVENING ST
CLUB, TFL, FASHION
ROYAL BALLET, ST P
BC, BEIGEL BAKE, CH
GORDON'S WINE BA
NIVERSITY COLLEGE
PAUL'S CATHEDRA
FORM CLUB, HER MA
SEUM, MADAME TU
AL BALLET, DORCHE
GE, NEW COVENT GA
ALLET, NATURAL HIS
RISTIES, UNIVERSITY
DIUM, LBC, TOWER B
ATS, EVENING STAN
HER MAJESTY'S T